CRISIS in SPADES...

One Man's Opinion

Sam Landau

PUBLISHED BY LULU DISTRIBUTION SERVICES

Copyright © 2007 by Sam Landau

ISBN: 978-1-4303-2276-4

All right reserved.

www.lulu.com

First printing: July 2007

Printed in the U.S.A.

To my wife for her enduring patience, her understanding, and her great work in converting my original written manuscript into acceptable printed format for publishing.

I also wish to express my appreciation to Ronnie Smith of Ocala, Florida for reviewing and editing my work. Her assistance proved to be invaluable.

TABLE OF CONTENTS
PROLOGUE

PART III – THE IMMIGRATION CRISIS

PART IV – OUR HEALTH CARE DILEMMA

PROLOGUE
OUR GREAT NATION

The nation we live in is a veritable melting pot of humanity. People of every race, every creed, and every color make up our great society. It is a democracy – but it is no utopia. We are a free people guided by the laws we ourselves have established to live by.

We have never had imperialistic designs on other nations. Our battles have been predicated upon our concern for all humanity. We do not fight to increase our property or to enslave our fellow man. We fight to secure our way of life. We are a compassionate people. We believe in assisting others in their plight to enjoy a life free of indignities and injustices.

As I understand it, we are considered one of the most populous nations in the world.

Economically, we produce roughly a third of the world's goods and services, and our military is considered one of the most, if not the most, powerful in the world.

We are, as political scientist, Seymour Martin Lipset writes, "The most religious, optimistic, patriotic, rights oriented and individualistic country in the world. At the same time, however, we are also the most materialistic, self-absorbed and swaggering nation on earth."

Even in this great benevolent society of America, man has often succumbed to evil traits. I prefer to refer to this as our dark side. We have not, and are not, always so magnanimous, virtuous, noble and morally upright. Only too often our moral turpitude and codes are not all that they are purported to be.

Centuries of racism, Indian warfare, race riots, agrarian uprisings, frontier vigilantism and industrial conflicts are all excused as exceptions to the perceptions of Americans as being peaceful and law abiding – essentially, a non-violent people! The brutality and suffering promulgated even after our Civil War by unsavory scoundrels continued to mar this perception.

"The 1950's gave us one of the most violent decades in US history, replete with massive urban riots outbursts of radical antagonism, a presidential assassination and other notable assassinations, campus violence, anti-war disorder, and a spectacular increase in crime and homicide rates."[1] All this committed by a non-violent people!

How then, does a nation of immigrants, coming to this country to escape persecution, injustice, bigotry and prejudice, end up with a history of radical strife and bigotry with large companies guilty of greed, injustice, corruption and obsessions with power – power, which adversely affects the lives of so many people?

Let us take a peak in retrospect at some of this racial strife, bigotry, corruption and injustice that we have been partisan to, and remain guilty of, to this day.

PART I

OUR RACIAL CRISIS IN RETROSPECT

Early Explorers and Colonists

Early European explorers (Drake, Cortez, Hawkins and others) ravaged the shores of the American continents seeking gold, silver and other plunders. They sought to enslave the natives who were terrified into submission by soldiers on horseback armed with death dealing weapons and powerful cannons – all of which were totally foreign to the natives. The explorers conquered and destroyed whole villages and peoples with ruthless abandon.

The early settlers who colonized the New England area were known as Pilgrims. They were a well-organized, tightly knit group. They came here seeking a radical departure from both the church and government of England. They sought to restore authority to the church and to purify it from the corruption they deplored.

The laws governing personal conduct were very strict. One had to be "certified" before being admitted to the congregation and to the community as a citizen. Deviation from church practices, doctrine, procedures and principles were just not tolerated! The smallest infraction of their rules/laws would demand harsh treatment or prison and, in too many cases, even death, i.e., Plymouth – Salem etc. It's almost as though these settlers who came here to escape tyranny and injustice turned right around and displayed practically the same injustice in the colonies. Fear and trepidation prevailed and many settlers began to move south to experience greater freedom.

The Native American

Initially, the early settlers attempted to use the provisions (food etc.) they salvaged from their trips. When they were forced to forage for themselves from their surroundings they, of course, experienced some difficulty. The Indians taught them how to grow vegetables. They shared their corn with the settlers and assisted with the hunt. But, most of the settlers were not satisfied with meager provisions – so, they began to take from the Indian, more than was given – thus hostility began to settle in.

The American Indians had a reverence for Mother Earth and wildlife species. They were very frugal in their hunt, killing only what they would use to eat, clothe or shelter themselves. There were, of course, exceptions, but not many.

As our forefathers increased in number, moving west, they "settled in" building farms, ranches, homes and then towns and cities. The impact on what was once Indian land was, of course, devastating to the Indians. The environmental ecology and bio diversity no longer flourished. The Indians had no one to turn to for help or appeal – the teaming masses of the "white man" were overwhelming. The US cavalry, of course, provided more than their share of difficulty – which was their job – to protect the settlers. The Indian was recognized then as a "savage" to be dealt with accordingly. The outraged Indian fought to the death to preserve his threatened way of life – increasingly to no avail.

The Constitution of the United States gave the congress plenary power over Indian affairs to make treaties and to acquire land for a growing population and for westward expansion. The American Indians fought relentlessly to embrace their culture to follow in the footsteps of their ancestors.

Over 372 treaties were written, but few of them were lived up to. One way or another, we managed to break most of them. The Indian, although a party to the treaties, had no real rights.

For the Plains Indian, the vast herds of bison (buffalo) provided good hunting. It was a way of life for them in which the bison provided food and hides for clothing and shelter. "Historians of the West frequently point out that the Plains Indian was not defeated by the US Cavalry but by the destruction of the buffalo"[2] by early white explorers, fur traders and other settlers often killing more than they needed.

The Indian Chief Seattle expressed this concept in 1887, "Every part of this country is sacred to my people. Every hillside, every valley, every plain and every grove have been hallowed by some fond memory or some sad experience of my tribe. Even the rocks, which seem to lie dumb as they swelter in the sun along the silent shore in solemn grandeur, thrill with memories of past events connected with the fate of my people."[3]

The real tragedy took place with the massacre of the buffalo from 1870 to 1883. The buffalo was hunted for sport as well as hides to the point of virtual extinction. It would be difficult to imagine the thoughts of the Indian as he observed the slaughter and waste while Buffalo Bill became a hero. Hunger, disease and despair prevailed.

"A quarter of a million American Indians were confined to reservations. But the reservation systems, while well-meaning, all too often operated as a corrupt and cruel machine that failed to maintain the Indian at a decent level of sustenance or to provide elementary sanitation."[4]

The American Indian became identified as a U.S. citizen in 1924. However, it took until 1948 for the Arizona State Supreme Court to rule that the American Indian had voting rights.

Time Magazine printed an article in January 2004, claiming that the US mismanaged the oil and gas legacies it promised to protect. Essentially, land was given to the Native Indians by the Department of the Interior's local B.I.A. agent and promised that any profits from the property would be held in trust for its owners.

However, the owners received relatively little of the monies coming to them. The money had been mismanaged or stolen from accounts held in trust since the late 19th century. The Indians were not allowed to see the accounts and given just enough to subsist. For example, the total paid over many years to one Indian Tribe, $35,000; should actually have been well over $70 million. There just doesn't seem to have been an end to our greed and our injustices to the Native Americans.

The African American

Historically, our treatment of the African American has been nothing short of appalling. It is a tragic tale of racism and a tale of dehumanization – a tale of a people fraught with fear, insecurity and humiliation. It is a tale of a great people treated as property, as chattel, as slaves, rather than as a terrorized and intimidated, people forced to submit to the shameful bigoted and prejudicial criminal justice system of the time. It is a tale of people restricted to "coloreds only" facilities (schools, restaurants, theaters and churches) and required to sit apart from white folks in buses, trains, etc. Here in a free, democratic country they were denied inherent rights to life, liberty and the pursuit of happiness.

The institution of slavery first took place in this country back in the 1600s, but it became prevalent in the northern and southern states during the 19th century.

While the 13th Amendment of 1865 (the Emancipation Proclamation) ended slavery, the black Americans were not yet permitted to vote. The Civil Rights Act of 1866 enabled the black American to go where he wanted, to move at will, to plant his own garden, to choose a new name, if desired, to practice his own religion and to go to school and learn. Congress then passed a Reconstruction Act, permitting the black American to vote "at last".

Still the black American was mistreated – singled out and terrorized for no other reason, other than to suppress, to discourage, and in so many ways, prohibit the black American from participating and enjoying a normal way of life.

Lynch mobs acted, not to punish but, to instill fear in the African American occupied communities, resulting in almost 3,000 African Americans being lynched in the south between 1892 and 1903.

The organization known as the Klu Klux Klan, with their white masks and hoods, terrorized the black people. They continue to do so to this day. However, they do not confine their malice to the black communities but to anyone who cannot claim Anglo-Saxon, Christian origins – Jew, Roman Catholic and Negro, bombings, shootings, stabbings, fires and the like characterize their evil actions.

It is interesting to note that so many of these so called Klan members are educated people. One can only conclude from this that these people are in some way disturbed or demented – that their diabolical mind sets have been warped.

It is difficult to understand how these Klan people rationalize their behavior in view of the inspiring testimony and tremendous contributions these African American people have made to our country. Black Americans certainly have a heritage to be proud of. Just let the Klan attempt to deny the contributions of Booker T. Washington, Rosa Parks, Frederick Douglas, Martin Luther King, Shirley Chisholm, Dorothy Dandridge, Ella Fitzgerald, Jimi Hendrix, Duke Ellington, Louis Armstrong, Joe Louis, Sara Breedlove Walker, Jesse Jackson and Ray Charles.

And so many other notable, successful black Americans not to mention the successful black stars in baseball, football, track and basketball and what about our movie stars. What say you Mr. Klansman? Are these people all inferior to you? All of them are black Americans and all of them successful in education, science, arts, literature, politics, medicine and sports!

Hispanic Americans

Other forms of racial discrimination occurred with the immigration of Hispanics from Mexico into our South and West during the 1890's. "This considerable influx of Mexican people resulted in the swelling of Mexican communities throughout the southwest, changing the character of Mexican life in the U.S."[5]

Hispanic children with a language barrier were considered inferior and somewhat retarded or learning disabled so they were placed into lower level classes, non-academic classes, and given general educational and vocational courses. Discrimination was very evident. The establishment of Puerto Rican colonies was similar to that of the Mexican immigrant colonies and resulted in a continuation of the colonial experience.

"This feeling was exacerbated even more when they encountered rejection in this country. In the so-called Harlem riots in July 1926, Puerto Ricans were attacked by non-Hispanics as their numbers were becoming larger in Manhattan neighborhoods."[6]

Hispanics are a fast growing major group of people in this country. The Labor Department's Bureau of Labor Statistics projects that the Hispanic segment of the population in the United States is fast becoming larger than the black segment.

Our mistreatment of minorities is historical – while America represents the melting pot of civilization, it is difficult to understand how, even to this day, this blatant racial discrimination continues – seemingly unchecked. Is it so hard for some people to fathom the concept that we are not black people, not yellow people, not red people, not Latin people, not Jews, not Catholics... but, we are American's. Our color and choice of a particular religious faith is a personal matter – "not a label".

Congress needs to pass some new laws to deal with the kind of prejudice demonstrated by the skinheads, the neo-Nazis and others who deal in their own particular brand of terrorism. I'd like to hear them tell some famous black athletes, movie stars, mayors, police chiefs, writers, lawyers, doctors, etc. – that they are inferior! These racist groups can no longer be tolerated. They breed social injustice crime, intolerance, prejudice and evil of every description.

PART II
RADICAL CHANGES AND CHALLENGES

Our Global Community

It has been said that... "Man is evolutionary and science is revolutionary." A serious gap of time occurs which generally becomes a major problem. Man, historically has had difficulty coping and adjusting to this gap and to the revolutionary and traumatic changes it precipitates.

Science and technology have been advancing at a phenomenal pace. This is the high tech era... the era of nanotechnology with stem cell research, sophisticated computer applications, holograph technology, space age, medical technology, micro-engineering, earthquake forecasting, metallurgical and chemical developments and many other innovative accomplishments which have changed our very way of life. It has radically changed the fields of education, medicine, energy, biological and technological warfare and, today, the relative ease with which the fanatical terrorist, now threaten our lives.

This spiraling panorama of space age technology has impacted the entire world we live in. It has caused our world as we know it, to virtually shrink through global communication, transportation and technology in general. It has opened the door to more diversity of life styles and beliefs and our relations with other nations.

Saul Alinsky, in his work, "Rules for Radicals" [1971] wrote: "Change means movement. Movement means friction. Only in the frictionless vacuum of a non-existent abstract world can movement or change occur without the abrasive friction of conflict." It is also apparent that the community we live in today is a "global community". We are no longer immune from the problems of other nations and other people regardless of how remote they may seem to be. We no longer have the option to live in isolation without regard to what's taking place elsewhere.

The United States as a global power, however, has been challenged. Other nations are gaining in economic and political stature. As a prime example – China! Yet, the United States still maintains its preeminence with its vast natural resources, modern industrial plants and its educated population – it is still a superpower.

The world must open its eyes to see clearly that we can no longer live in isolation. Nations must respect each other, enabling all nations to live and conduct themselves as they see fit. However, it must be understood that no nation, nor any people within any nation, shall be permitted to bring terror or disarray to any other nation. This means that schools throughout the world that teach hatred, death and terror others cannot be tolerated. It's like permitting a school here in the United States to outwardly teach hatred of the Jews, hatred of the blacks, hatred of the Latin's and the overthrow of our government. We would not permit it.

The world's population now stands at roughly six billion. In the next one- half century, the total will increase by three billion. Ninety-five percent of this growth will occur in developing countries. These areas will be teaming with poor and resentful children. We must educate these children to protect them from any prejudice and hatred, which might filter down from misguided parents.

On September 11, 2001, this country was dealt a disastrous awakening here at home base, by some disturbed, misguided patriots of hell. We no longer can afford to live independently from rest of the world (not that we really ever could). Today, we have to realize that we live in a global society – no longer immune from physical attack simply because of a vast ocean separating our continent from others. Revenge and retaliation unfortunately are quite naturally considered justified by some nations; and can easily run amok and become a global crisis that will very quickly lead to our demise.

Our Global Challenges

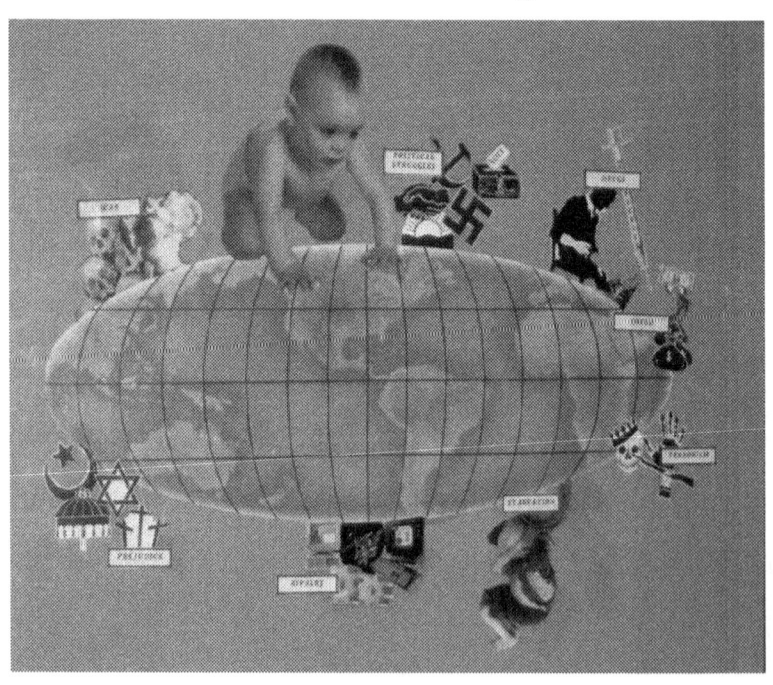

The Outlook

The Fallibility of Man

Man is considered as an incredibly magnificent biological creature.   However, the emotional and behavioral characteristics of our psyche are capable of being twisted, torn, distorted and otherwise tossed out of kilter.

Throughout history, since the beginning of time, this susceptible psyche (phenomenon) has resulted in men of violence, of greed, of intemperance and of men who deal in prejudice, in hatred and in other forms of evil.

Taken in historical retrospect, we could go back to the Roman Empire and consider the persecution of Christians. Or consider the inhuman treatment of the black slaves during the 18-19th centuries, slave trade on English ships prior to its eventual abolition in England.

Or more recently in history, we would consider the atrocities committed by Nazi Germany and it's Gestapo in World War II. Here, they attempted to annihilate the Jews and others in Europe. Consider, as well, the unprecedented attack on us at

Pearl Harbor. Of course, there are numerous other acts of brutal treatment and terror we could cite from history.

Certainly the disaster and violence in Sudan's Darfur region in Africa with fighting between rebels and government forces which has killed more than 200,000 people, serves as a glaring illustration currently.

In the Sudan an ethnically Arab rebel militia group known as Jan Jaweed has been terrorizing the non-Arab Africans and Christians since early 2003.

There are two groups, the Sudan Liberation Army and its smaller counterpart, the Justice and Equality Movement. The hostilities these groups have invoked have caused over one million non-Arab Africans to become refugees. These displaced people lack adequate food and shelter. Their villages were attacked, men and boys were killed, women raped, people tortured and burned to death, crops destroyed, livestock and homes burned. Hunger and disease have killed up to 50,000 of them.

The UN has called Darfur (a devastated swath of Western Sudan) the world's most humanitarian crisis and said it has claimed over 70,000 lives. Colin Powell has placed the blame squarely on the Sudanese government and the allied Arab Jan Jaweed militias, referring to the action as genocide.

The United Nations recognizes the atrocities and acknowledges the United States proposal in the UN Security Council to impart sanctions against Sudan. It has, however, made little progress. It would appear that opposition to any UN action came from two prominent nations that coincidently are currently importing Sudanese oil… this does sound vaguely familiar!

On Tuesday, November 9, 2004, Nat Hentoff, a newspaper enterprise association writer, wrote about another atrocity. This one in Uzbekistan (a state under the ferocious rule of Islam Karimov) where various forms of inhuman torture were prevailing, including boiling a human being in oil! Nat Hentoff states it well, "Ignoring the screams of the horrifically tortured doesn't keep our hands from being stained with their blood". This, of course, applies equally to the atrocities in Sudan and elsewhere.

Someone once said that, "Man should see a little clearer and judge less harshly what he cannot see." Man's inhumanity to man cannot be tolerated, particularly in this age of technological sophistication. There can be no accommodation for this kind of evil. The stakes are entirely too high!

The Mid-East Crisis

The Mid-East has been a veritable caldron of bloody unrest for centuries. Since time immemorial, the land of the Bible: Israel, Jordan, Lebanon, Syria, Iraq, Saudi Arabia, Egypt and Iran have been a land of turmoil and radical conflict.

For thousands of years biblical scholars and archaeologists alike have worked feverishly, debating and hotly contesting the reliability and authenticity of historical claims. Numerous stories and written works describing the plight of ancient Israelites have been published. Reality or myth, we cannot be sure. But we cannot overlook the importance of buried history and there is a great deal of it buried in the sands of the Mid-East.

Israel and the Palestinians

This very land was the birthplace of Christianity and the Muslims alike. The history of the Jews, the Christians, and the Muslims all share in this heritage but, only too often, refuse to admit it.

In 1917 Palestine was established as a national home for the Jewish people by the British Bal Four Declaration. In 1922 the United Nations entrusted Britain with a mandate for Palestine.

The nationhood of the "Palestinians" is a myth. The reality is that the concept of "Palestinians" is one that did not exist until about 1948 (the time of the proclamation of the State of Israel.) Prior to that time, the Jews were the Palestinians.

We hear so much about the so-called Palestinian refugees claim that they have the right to return to, what they call, their homeland... Israel. Actually few of these people ever lived in Israel before. They are, in fact, the children and grandchildren of those who fled willingly in 1948!

The ideology of the Palestinians of today and most Arabs is the complete disappearance of Israel – its annihilation. They do not recognize Israel as a state nor do they acknowledge that the Jewish people are indigenous to the land but rather suggest that they are just a bunch of trespassers passing through.

Arab children are brought up, from an early age, with a mortal hatred against Israeli's and the Jews. These children are even taught to believe in the promise of unimaginable pleasures if they sacrifice themselves in the holy cause of killing Jews. As a result, of course, Israelis and the Palestinians have now been in conflict with each other for over 50 years – terrorism is a way of life.

Israel has been terrorized and under constant attack with over 20,000 dead in defensive wars. Yet they have created a social and political system and a thriving economy that has astounded people throughout the world.

Many formulas for settlement have been proposed. Many meetings have been held but none have reached fruition. The Palestinian leaders have made it clear that their ultimate aim is not to impose their will on the people of Israel but rather to destroy them and take their place. Efforts to meet peacefully and negotiate productively usually end in futility. Israel has repeatedly shown its willingness to yield land, to share and to negotiate a mutually beneficial agreement. However, every time a settlement appears promising, the Palestinians invariably strike again with another act of atrocity.

Then, each time Israel attempts to retaliate in their own defense, their efforts are viewed as aggressive and villainous. Where deaths and injuries resulted particularly with innocent children the Israelis were considered at fault. It is the old story of which came first – the chicken or the egg. The media, unfortunately, rarely favors the Israelis as though the Israelis have no right to protect themselves. The U.N. has been of no use whatsoever – once even being accused of becoming the leading global purveyor of anti-Semitism.

The Palestinians are known to use unsavory tactics involving men, women and even children placed in hospitals, schools and holy religious schools and then firing weapons on the Israelis from these buildings– knowing that the Israelis would be reluctant to retaliate. The Palestinians use children in front lines of city streets to fire upon the Israelis, then, when an Israeli retaliates, a Palestinian child is killed and they use this as propaganda, making the Jews appear as monsters deserving severe condemnation.

Yasser Arafat is now deceased. It is, therefore, not appropriate to desecrate his memory. It is necessary, however, to point out that, while in power, he violated every agreement he entered into with the Israelis and poisoned the minds of two generations of Palestinian Arabs against Israel and the Jews.

The United States continues to lend support to the Israeli cause. Many of the conferences and negotiations that have taken place have been due to the efforts of the United States to bring about a reasonable peace plan. But, of course, political duplicity negates virtually every effort to reach a unilateral agreement.

We assisted the Israelis and then in 1990 we engaged in combat in the Persian Gulf and in the Balkan, coming to the aid of Bosnia and Kosovo.

As a nation, we have been envied for our wealth, success and power. Most of the Arab world, however, despises us as purveyors of secularism – they revile us as enemies of Islam – thus alienating us from the Arab world.

Throughout the Middle East and in many other parts of the world, mortal hatred against Israel and against Americans is taught to children of all ages. In many areas of the Islamic world impressionable, economically deprived young boys are kept entirely ignorant of the world.

They are encouraged to kill, to revere Allah and hate Americans and to prepare for martyrdom. They are given only one interpretation of the Koran – twisted, distorted and misleading, to justify their hatred, terror and killing. Hatred of Israel and against the Jews is strong and abiding and virulent – hatred against the Americans is equally strong, abiding and virulent.

Our Rude Awakening – Afghanistan

On September 11, 2001, the World Trade Center and the Pentagon were attacked. The World Trade Center was destroyed and thousands of innocent men, women and children of many different races and beliefs were killed.

For a nation that has, for two centuries, felt safe at home, it was a momentous rude awakening – an atrocious act of sheer depravity by only a few fanatical, disturbed and misguided patriots of hell. But the realization that we now live in a global society, a global economy, no longer immune from physical attack, simply because we are separated from other continents by the oceans, became alarmingly crystal clear!

Once it was clear that Osama Bin laden of Afghanistan was responsible, we retaliated quickly by declaring war on Afghanistan. The first 100 days witnessed the single most important victory ever in the war on terrorism: the conquest of Afghanistan, the installation of a pro-American government, and the decimating and/or scattering of al-Qaida. When the President declared war, he declared war not just on terrorists, but on states as well – states that harbor terrorists, states that aid and abet terrorism, states that hunger for weapons of mass destruction (WMD). Unfortunately Osama Bin Laden is still at large hidden somewhere in the mid-East region – we know not where!

Bin Laden blames the U.S. for the killing of "innocents" by American and Israeli forces, although he ignores the attacks on innocents by the "PLO" and other terrorist friends. Bin Laden wants the U.S. to end its support of Israel so his enemies could invade and eliminate the nation altogether. Bin Laden takes full responsibility for the 9/11 attack on us. Despite the years on the run, Bin Laden as head of al-Qaida remains a threat. Bin Laden truly believes Islam could beat the West, thus his efforts to polarize the world into Islam and the West.

Afghanistan is a country roughly 33% larger than Iraq with about 15% more population. For the most part, it's a very hostile, volatile, high-risk environment. Its people are only too vulnerable to Taliban control. They have no major water project no power project and lots and lots of barren, dry, sandy desert. Efforts; however, are currently underway to construct electric, water and power plants in Afghanistan. Of course, the Taliban is making every effort to prevent this.

Numerous terrorist roadside and suicide bombs continuously rock the country sides. In the Kandahar province we find the Taliban's heartland and the Opium trade and its production is at an all-time high.

Our Pre-Emptive Strike – Iraq

Iraq was a rogue state controlled by the tyrant Saddam Hussein – guilty of unspeakable crimes against humanity. The Iraqi nation was suffering. Starvation was prevalent under this cruel and corrupt dictator.

The United States and other nations in our global community became concerned that Iraq was harboring biological and other weapons of mass destruction. The threat of unconventional weapons getting into the hands of other rogue states or terrorists presented a serious international security challenge. The threat may or may not have been imminent, but it was ominous and likely inevitable in time.

Every effort was made to solicit the aid and cooperation of a coalition of nations through the United Nations. While a number of nations went along with the coalition effort, a few (key) nations who could have assisted refused to do so because of their eagerness to pursue economic self-interests with Saddam Hussein.

A United Nations inspection team was charged with locating weapons of mass destruction in Iraq. They found nothing. It was a fruitless search. If Saddam had not actually destroyed whatever weapons he may have had, he would most assuredly, have made every effort to move the weapons (biological or otherwise) out of Iraq – he was no fool; whether or not the original intelligence was shoddy, remains to be seen.

In the October 2004 issue of Time magazine, there appeared an article by Daniel Eisenberg entitled "WMD Myth or Reality", the article encapsulated the central conclusion of the newly issued "Duelfer Report". It compared, in succinct terms, what we thought then as opposed to our thoughts reconsidered!

Acting in good faith, based upon the intelligence provided at the time, that Saddam Hussein harbored weapons of mass destruction, we, the United States, decided upon a pre-emptive attack on Iraq.

Despite the fact that we had captured Saddam, the war in Iraq persisted. It is not, however, the nation of Iraq we are still at war with… it is with the terrorists supported by other radical Muslim allied nations whom we refer to as "insurgents". These insurgents have no intention of laying down their arms. They are making every effort to prevent Iraq's recover. The insurgents are trying to turn the resistance into an international Jihad (holy war) movement.

While we are attempting to establish a peaceful democratic government in Iraq, the insurgents continue to use every means possible to prevent us from doing so. The suicide car bombs, the mortars, the rockets and the destruction of property and lives remain a daily occurrence in Iraq.

Now we are faced with what may be a termed a "global intifada" – which threatens and certainly challenges our security and our global community.

Other Conflicts – Lebanon

The conflict between Israel and the Hezbollah was triggered by the capture by the Hezbollah's of two Israel soldiers. Negotiations between the two for release of the captives involving prisoner swaps were fruitless. Israel considered the exchange rate totally unreasonable – responded by bombing a part of Beirut's International Airport – thus began the exchange of missiles, rockets and bombs of every description – retaliation was swift!

It is believed that the war was deliberately provoked by Iran and Syria via the terrorist organization, Hezbollah and Hamas whose aim it is to obliterate the Jews from this part of the world.

Civilians on both sides endured hardships but seemingly the people along the border in Lebanon where most of the action took place endured more severe losses.

I do not believe the Israeli captive was ever released.

The Geneva Convention, which forbids concealing weapons among civilians, is exactly what the Hezbollah was doing. Israeli forces didn't know that dozens of innocent civilians have found refuge in the very location of the Hezbollah, guns, missiles, etc. This was the way the Hezbollah fought, placing their armaments behind civilians in their homes and health facilities and the like. Of course, when Israelis responded to the fire from these locations, they believed they were firing upon the enemy's guns emplacements, not aware of the civilians there; thus the cries of Israelis killing innocent civilians, when Israel was acting in good faith in self-defense. The critics of Israel were employing a double standard saying nothing about the attacks on innocent Israeli civilians.

Israel artillery barrage misfired and killed (unintentionally) 19 people. But Israel fired this barrage to stop militants from launching rockets into Israel. Why is it always okay for the Palestinians to shoot and kill but, when Israel responds, this is considered unfair?

I've noticed some notes to the editor of various news magazines making rash statements such as "Israel has no right to inflict so much pain and suffering on innocent people"; "Failure to condemn Israel for heinous attacks on civilians", etc. Obviously these people are ill informed of the facts or simply just outright prejudiced.

The active war (hostilities) ended with an "empty" peace treaty. Negotiations were entered into, but not carried out. The UN proved useless in attempting to remove the Hezbollah from the area as agreed.

During the 34-day conflict, the border areas of Lebanon became a shamble of wreckage, homes and shattered streets. The Hezbollah is assisting the Lebanese men and women, young and old alike, – particularly the young men assisting with reconstruction. They are given every support by the Hezbollah, sweetened by contributions of hard cash to help the people of Lebanon recoup. It's only natural, therefore, for these young men and women who may have lost everything, including loved ones to turn their loyalty to the Hezbollah – thus adding to the ranks of the Hezbollah!

This consolidation of support for Hezbollah is preparing the way for it to become one of the most powerful forces in the region, which of course, makes it that much more difficult to disarm.

Other Conflicts – The Gaza Strip

Israel pulled out of Gaza well over two years ago (I believe in 2005). Elections were held and the hard line Hamas militants were elected to power thus splitting the Palestinians into two factions: the Hamas and the Fatahs. Virtual war broke out between the two factions with Israel right in the middle.

As far as the vast majority of elite Palestinians are concerned, the ideology of violence and hatred of Jews continues – labeling them "the enemy of Allah"! The hard line Hamas refuse to even recognize the existence of Israel and call for its destruction, whereas Abbas of the Fatah faction favor peace with the Israelis. The real crisis began when the militants of the Palestinians Islamists groups kidnapped an Israeli soldier.

Warlords, armed gangs and terrorists, none of which have anything even resembling a rule of law, rule the Palestinian monarchy. Tracking martyrdom to the children is commonplace. It is ingrained into the Palestinian culture.

The Hamas will not agree to end its violence. They are pledged to it, thus the forces of evil continue unabashed, as though they hold a free ticket to conduct terror.

Why is it we persist in negotiating with the likes of these people? Their warped frame of mind will not permit it. We know they have no intention of giving up their objective of destroying the Jews.

Hezbollah will continue with its aggression and Hamas with its aggression with the added threat of the al-Qaida with no apparent end in sight (Feb. 07)!

Impending Danger – Iran & North Korea

The country of Iran is well known as a major sponsor of terrorism. It has opposed virtually every U.S. backed peace initiative in the Middle East and has been included in President Bush's "Axis of Evil". It is and has been decidedly anti-American… known to be implicated in more than one terrorist attack on Americans.

Iran has been found to be involved in nuclear technology related to uranium enrichment, a technology that can produce a nuclear fuse or atomic weapons. Iran, of course, contends that it is pursuing nuclear technology for peaceful means.

In fact, Iran's new Shehab-3 missile has a range of 800 miles and could reach anywhere in the Middle East and most of Europe. Iran has vast oil and gas resources. The pretense of pursuing nuclear power solely for peaceful purposes must be viewed with suspicion.

To date (Feb. 07), Iran has not agreed to any curtailment but, to the contrary, is promoting the fact that it is going ahead with its uranium enrichment program without concern.

To complicate the issue, Iran is not prohibited from enriching uranium under its obligations to the nuclear non-proliferation treaties, but it is barred from arms-related work and uranium enrichment activities. Any agreements entered into in this regard should likewise be viewed with caution and subject to stringent controls.

Joining Iran in the proverbial "Axis of Evil" is North Korea – another very dangerous threat and another crisis!

Kim Jong III of North Korea is a tyrant and he is starving his people. He is pursuing nukes and is well down the road to making some. North Korea has tested a missile that could deliver a nuclear warhead to the United States or he could sell some of his stock to terrorists.

At one time, Kim Jong III had thrown out inspectors and accelerated his plutonium production. North Korea is thought to have one or two bombs and fuel for up to six of them.

A united front with Russia, Japan and South Korea was set up to negotiate with Kim Jong but he didn't budge. Here again, like Iran, the North Koreans claim peaceful pursuits with their atomic production – not to be used for hostile purposes!

The Challenge of China

And… lest we neglect to consider China, a nation of over 1.3 billion citizens, a growing military power extremely important in our strategic relations with other nations. Economically in our global community, it is already now becoming a major force to deal with in the industrial and business community of our nation.

The challenge is to maintain powerful relations with this huge empire. We must avoid at all costs, anything in our relations with China which would or could place this nation on a collision course with us… it would be disastrous. On the other hand, a more democratic and peaceful China could become mutually profitable for both nations. This is putting our crisis with China succinctly.

Breeding Evil – The Fanatic Terrorist

Today we face the fanatic terrorist – a ruthless enemy who seeks to destroy our values and our civic order – our very way of life. This fanatic is depraved. He rejoices in the murder of men, women and children of so many different races and beliefs.

We are at war with these terrorists but it's a different kind of war. We have never been called upon to face an enemy with neither front lines nor any defining boundaries, an enemy who cannot be reasoned with; nor does he value life itself, as we know it.

It's a far different kind of warfare, calling for "high tech" weapons and information technology. It's a war fought with small, highly trained, readily adaptable units. We are faced with coping with an enemy far different from us.

Let's first distinguish between a terrorist and an insurgent, since we hear so much about both of them. An insurgent is one who rises up against established authority and rebels against it. The terrorist, on the other hand, is, as used in this particular case, a religious fanatic – totally dedicated to his cause. He will not surrender, and will have to be captured or killed. These terrorists and the people who support them must be dissuaded.

While there are exceptions, most terrorists are poor and impressionable boys kept entirely ignorant of the world, and for that matter, largely ignorant of all but one interpretation of Islam. It is also possible they may have witnessed the death of a loved one during a battle or an attack by an opposing force. Possibly involving the American military in which case, the hatred becomes deep set and embedded in the very fiber of their being.

These young men generally range in age from 8 to 35, drawn from the dire poor. Tuition and room and board are free, funded by wealthy Pakistanis and other devout, politically-minded Muslims in the Persian Gulf countries. "There are one million students studying in Pakistan's 10,000 or so madrassas, and militant Islam is at the core of most of these schools."[7]

"Students memorize the Koran. High school and college age students are enrolled in an eight-year course of study in interpretation of the Koran and the Hadith, a narration of the life and sayings of the Profit Muhammad, Islamic jurisprudence, and Islamic history. There are no courses in world history, math, computers or science."[8] They are taught to revere Allah, to embrace holy war, to hate America and to prepare for martyrdom. According to the theology taught at most madrassas schools, dying for Islam showers a host of blessings on the martyr, including a welcome to heaven.

The fanatic is intoxicated with hatred. These fanatics are ideologically driven. At its core, Islam is moderate and tolerant of others but they maintain that the West compels Muslims to live under the control of infidels. Ben Laden claims to want to keep Islam pure from the pollution of these infidels...us!

"The purpose of the terrorists we encounter is to manipulate, to increase the pain of the victim's family and friends, to force western governments to moderate their opposition to terrorist networks and to panic foreigners into leaving Muslim land."[9]

Their objective is clear – to obtain and use, if necessary, nuclear weapons as a way of dictating terms to a world society that no longer tolerates crimes against humanity.

To fight fanaticism, we must first fight indifference to evil… we fight indifference with <u>education</u>.

Raging Racism

The vast majority of the world's more than one billion practicing Muslims are peaceful citizens getting on with their lives. The true Muslim believes in restoring pure religious law as formulated by the prophet, Mohammed. The foundation of the law is, of course, belief in Allah as the one true god.

The moderate Muslim renounces terror, violence and intolerance as incompatible with the faith. Whereas, the radical Muslims consider themselves righteous warriors engaged in a holy war against Satan.

Islamic moderates want to believe Muslims can co-exist peacefully with people of other faiths or of no faith at all and they do so every day throughout this world. Unfortunately, the number of Muslims espousing radical belief is growing.

Withstanding the other ramifications of the attacks on Afghanistan and Iraq, one thing is certain; they infuriated the radical Muslim element, increased their anger, and gave them added fuel to ferment their fire of hatred and retribution against Americans – the so-called infidels, sowing the seeds of hatred. Even some of the more modern democratic and peace loving Muslims have some ambivalent feelings – American presence is perceived as an attack on Islam.

In other parts of the world the virus of anti-Semitism is running amok unchecked by feeble political leadership. "From Kiev in the East to Balboa and Barcelona in Spain and some in the South, from Marseilles to Paris to Berlin in the West, the poison is at work."[10] The summary of evil deeds can only sketch the daily nightmare. Jews and people presumed to be Jews are assaulted across the region. Attackers shouting racist slogans, throw stones at school children, at worshippers leaving religious services, at Rabbis, Jewish homes, schools and synagogues are firebombed, windows are smashed, scores of Jewish cemeteries are desecrated with anti-Jewish slogans and threats and Nazi symbols scrawled on walls and monuments. In London, a young student reading Psalms is stabbed 27 times on a city bus. Most of this is predicated upon the rejection of Israel as an equal member of the family of nations.

No "band-aid" will rectify these atrocities – no condemnation – no fine or national sanction will do it either. The only solution (granted somewhat idealistic), is to strike at the core of the problem – the misinformation, lies, twisted and disturbed truths fed to the children and young adults. They have no idea of what is right or wrong other than what they have been taught by their parents, tutors, guardians and leaders.

The plight of Israel and the Jewish people and others living in Israel has been threatened relentlessly for a good many years now. The Israelis have continually sought peace. They have offered to share the land and to live in peace and harmony. However, the fundamental premise of the Arab/ Palestinian justifications for their actions remains the same – their prime motivation is the total annihilation of Israel as such and of all the Jews residing there.

On that basis, only the unveiling and dissemination and the enlightenment and education of the Arab people, with historical fact, could possibly offer any hope. They must be made to understand that peace and cooperation are possible with the Jewish people but not with lies and deceit and treachery underfoot.

In Saudi Arabia alone, the world's largest financier of fundamental Islam, the kingdom government, pours millions into the establishment of Wahhabi, schools and mosques to spread their intolerance and anti-Semitic creed.

"The Saudis' schools support more than 30,000 of their schools and mosques in Saudi Arabia, Pakistan, Indonesia, Afghanistan, Western Europe and the United States. Wahhabi schools call for the destruction of the U.S. and Israel and Western values!"[11]

All too often, these children are misguided. They are taught to distrust and to hate other men. They have been bottle fed on false philosophical or theological doctrine totally out of context with reality and truth. Thus, man has created the kind of warped thinking that permeates our planet today in so many places. In the Mid-East, Ireland, Scotland and Africa, joblessness, often accompanied by resentment and simple boredom, serve as fertile recruiting ground for Islamic extremists.

Often, seemingly innocent clubs or after school Koran classes taught by Saudi-trained "Islam's" provide misinformation. These children and young men and women come from households where religion is an obscured cultural matter. They are easily seduced by the austere Wahhabi-Salafist vision of a global community of the faithful living under strict Islamic law. Attracted by this moral absolution, some are even drawn to the violent ways of the Jihadist.

Even the U.N. attempted to patch up the racial problem. They held a UN conference against racism, racial discrimination, xenophobia and related intolerance. Conceived in 1997, it was an honest effort typified by the political jargon and rhetoric characteristic of UN discussions. It was a disgrace in execution – nothing further of any consequence materialized.

The P.L.O., the Hamas, the Hezbollah, the Taliban, al-Qaida and other radical Muslim fanatic terrorist groups cannot survive without support. The regimes who have supported these groups are Iraq, Pakistan, Syria, Iran, Arafat's

Palestinians and other Mid-East and Persian Gulf nations and political organizations.

In many parts of the world, the governments themselves are supporting these terrorists. These governments have become, themselves, embroiled in corruption with annual revenues of over two trillion dollars. Rest assured a good measure of that money goes to the terrorist organizations.

As an illustration, India's top outlaw controls a criminal network that reaches into 14 countries with an army of contract killers, smugglers and executioners at his command. His name is Daw-ood Ibrabim, a Muslim exile. Reports indicate that he has thrown in his lot with al Qaeda and other Jihadist. He is considered to be one of the world's most wanted terrorists.

As recently as mid-January of 2007, reports of and to the Taliban are filtering in that Pakistani agents support militants, Taliban sympathies are prevalent; i.e.: Pakistanis are actively supporting the Taliban… (There have been local reports of students from the Madrassas sent on suicide missions!)

In Afghanistan a large part of these revenues is generated from the Opium crops throughout the country.

It must be understood that these terrorists and terrorist schools are to be found throughout our known world from Central Asia to North Africa to South America and of course, the Mid-East, where the rule of law remains an abstract concept.

How does one delve into the psyche of these religious fanatics? What is it we can do to curb the spread of this violence?

These terrorists deal out death to all who oppose them and will commit suicide without hesitation, as they say, "In god's name". Whose god? Certainly *not* ours, not even the Muslims. Where is there a God who approves of merciless killing, murders, rape, etc. – certainly not the Muslims, it's not a part of the Islamic Koran.

These radicals are fast going out of control and it's not a simple case of the warped mind of a common criminal, its religious fanaticism and we must turn our attention first to the source of the problem – our children and the schools they attend.

"We cannot live in a perpetual state of heightened readiness which would impose unacceptable costs on our way of life."[12]   Peace must become the rallying cry of not just parties in the country – but of nations throughout the world. Nor can fruitless, empty, political rhetoric chockfull of mistrust and lies be productive, be it American, Arab or any other national political or religious sect.

A resolution will not come readily.   It will require the enthusiastic support of all nations working together unilaterally to perpetuate and safeguard all people throughout our planet from terror and the destruction of life as we know it and to avoid a global conflict and holocaust.

O Lord, I pray that I had a light in hand – one with a strong penetrating beam – one which would enable me to see through and to find what prompts some men to do the things they do – the evil things they do to other men; to see what fabric, what special ilk these mortal beings are made of. What is it they claim to gain, what reward, what satisfaction they seek in the suffering of other men – for no apparent reason other than the color of their skin or the particular path they choose to follow to reach you.

Here in our country we have our own hate groups – our own nasty bigots who are groomed and brainwashed into thinking they belong to a superior race. If they profess Christian ways, how do they claim to do so and abide by the commandment, "do unto others as you would have them do unto you?" Perhaps they were given a lesson as a child, an untruth, a warped, misguided lesson. That lesson, which began as a seed, and began to grow and fester, inciting them to the acts they commit today.

"Come on now! You kick out the gooks, the next thing you know, you have to kick out the chinks, the spicks, the spooks, the kikes and all that's going to be left is a couple of brain dead rednecks." *(A quote from Robin Williams, actor and comedian)*

An Idealistic Solution – One Man's Opinion

Man's inhumanity to man is nothing new. Man cannot seem to live and let live among this fellow man.

We are all human beings regardless of our race, color or creed. We live and breath alike, we all require food, water and shelter, and we all seek to protect our offspring. However, when we attempt to impose our particular race or color or creed upon another or force our way of life upon another, we invariably run into trouble. History is paved with the bloodshed of those who have tried to do so.

Today as never before, however, we face a dilemma which could climax in our ultimate demise. We are courting disaster which demands a change in our relationships with one another. We live in a global community which no longer permits isolation. Our advancements in and achievements in communication and technology, in general, no longer provide a safe harbor. Evidence of a safe harbor isolated with an ocean separating us from threatening radical elements, groups and/or nations across the globe, was soon to change. When we were attacked on 9/11, followed by our retaliation in Afghanistan and then followed not much later in time by our attack on Iraq.

Our attack on Iraq was an act we considered justified in committing. We were prompted by our desire to preserve our safety and security from a nation we felt was threatening our way of life with weapons of mass destruction. Right or wrong we acted in good faith based upon the intelligence provided to us at the time.

It was our hope to eliminate the threat and possibly establish a center for democracy in that part of the world. Over 3½ years have passed since we tore down the statue of Saddam Hussein in Iraq – supposedly representing the end of an evil era. Now (Feb. 07) this promise of freedom and democracy in Iraq appears to be a (sad joke) in a sad state of affairs.

Post war reconstruction, the rebuilding of Iraq was to begin. President Bush in 2002 gave the Defense Department, rather than the State Department, the responsibility for post war reconstruction in Iraq. Efforts to effectively manage the overall task have failed. It has become a fiasco. While some schools were rebuilt, some stores reopened – they failed again and again to deliver water, electricity and, most significantly, security. To date, violence in that post war peaceful democracy in Iraq has cost more than 600,000 Iraqis their lives. In 2003, tens of thousands of Iraqis protested the U.S. occupation of Baghdad. In effect we won a war but lost the peace.

Thus far, our nation has made massive investments in lives and money. Over 3,000 lives and 350 billion dollars, not to mention the investment of roughly 15 thousand personnel from other countries collectively, representing the coalition forces. Now with two wars, each longer than the U.S. involvement in WWII, we remain heavily involved and committed to cope with the continuing strife and horror of the Mid-East region. Our troops remain committed to their mission and they deserve our support.

In Iraq the Sunni and the Shiite forces are at war with one another. It's important to note that the Sunnis, who are loyal to Saddam, are in the minority in Iraq. They had control during Saddam's regime. They now want that control back and they are fighting for it.

Add to this the infusion of the insurgents whom we are confident are being trained and equipped by Iran. They are passing through Syria without difficulty or any restraint by the Syrians, causing further disruption and an increase in the existing hostility. Likewise, the Kurds in the north want independence from Turkey. If that isn't enough we have to add the bands of the al-Qaida who incite further violence now and the crime and corruption which is prevalent throughout Iraq, disrupting construction, security and the production and distribution of oil.

Insurgents in Iraq are now considered self-sustaining financially. By raising millions of dollars each year from oil smuggling, kidnapping, counterfeiting, corrupt charities and other crimes that the Iraq government seems unable to prevent.

To leave Iraq, of course, is to leave a safe harbor for the enemy and to deliver vast oil reserves for the enemy to use to finance their terror.

The struggle and terror continues throughout the Mid-East in the Gaza Strip with Hamas and Fatah, the Palestinians and the Israelis and in Lebanon with the Hezbollah attempting to regain a foothold in Lebanon as a center for their fierce brand of terror. The entire Mid-East is tied together inexplicably as a common problem.

The Palestinians and the radical Muslims do not want to recognize the existence of a Jewish home or a Jewish state of any size or geographical configuration. They want the Jews, all of them, exterminated! This, of course, does not lend itself well to any kind of negotiation.

The war in Iraq, the war in Afghanistan, the terror and tyranny in Africa and elsewhere, the threats from radical extremists and of course, the potential threat from the development of nuclear warheads by hostile nations who would in all probability use them to accomplish their end-all present a formidable crisis, one we cannot turn away from!

Envision for a moment; a mere infant sitting atop our global community, gazing down at what we call earth. The infant is, of course, totally unaware of the world he is entering into or what lies ahead. He is totally unaware of the challenges of life and the road ahead, paved with bigotry, hatred, prejudice, political, greed, corruption and terror which permeates our planet.

Ideological differences can be dealt with. However, today, we are faced with religious fanatics, principally Islamic extremists and radicals who are driven by hate and committed to the destruction, if not the elimination of all who oppose them; the "Jihadist" a dedicated, radical Muslim who, like Hitler, believes in "ethnic cleansing". Their radical ways remain, and anyone who opposes them is not to be tolerated. Most Muslims refer to them as infidels.

To compound the problem, we are faced with the tyrannical despots whose rule is absolute without any regard for freedom or peace. These are the rogue nations rising to power to threaten the world with their particular brand of poison.

In some of these nations it is the religious leader who really rules – the political leader is just a figurehead – who makes a lot of noise. These powerful heads use their power to influence those under their control to inspire loyalty, ferment hate and terror. Unfortunately, we are not always able to reach these religious leaders, much less deal with them. We, therefore, are often faced with trying to negotiate with a leader who is really not in a position to make a decision of any real consequence.

It is important to make clear in this writing the fact, as previously discussed, that the Muslim people throughout the world are not the terrorists – only the extreme radical element that chooses to declare war on those who ignore their way. Muslims are a peaceful people. In fact, the very tenets of the Muslim Koran do not hold to the distortions propagated by the radical elements. In fact, as I understand it this Koran is very much akin to the Old Testament of our Bible.

Powerful, radical, Muslim groups currently finance too many schools throughout the world. They are established to promote this radical cause. Muslims teaching laws and philosophy have been distorted to serve the radical cause. In fact, private Saudi citizens have been known to give millions of dollars to Sunni insurgents in Iraq.

A special study group was formed not long ago called the Iraq Study Group. The group consisted of a very impressive assembly of well-informed and well-qualified, professional people with the highest credentials. The group included bipartisan members of Congress, military officers, regional experts, academics and other high level government officers from America and abroad. The group was charged with finding a solution and making recommendations as to how best to resolve this situation. The Report Group was chaired by James A Baker, III and Lee H. Hamilton.

Here are a few highlights of the group's recommendations. The group recognized the complexity of the problems, which could not by any means simply be confined or isolated to Iraq.

In Iraq, of course, we are dealing with sectarian violence for control between the Sunnis and the Shiites. This is further complicated by the violence of the insurgents and the terrorists. It is likewise complicated by the interests of the Kurds in the north part of Iraq seeking independence. Crime and corruption are prevalent throughout Iraq. Of course we must also end the destructive influence and forces of al-

Qaida. Security is totally out of control and the Iraq people have yet (March 07) to accept full responsibility and the Iraq army is ill-equipped in personnel, logistics and support despite all our efforts – yet, they want us out of there!

As indicated earlier in this writing, all of the problems of the Mid-East are inextricably linked. For example: Syria, Lebanon, Iran, Israel, the entire region including the Palestinians and the Israelis (Jerusalem, Gaza and the West Bank, etc.)

The Report Group recommends supporting the unity and territorial integrity of Iraq. The group recommends that we go on a diplomatic offensive – that we encourage national reconciliation. It suggests that the US build an international consensus for stability in Iraq and this region with an international support structure. The Iraqi people must become self-reliant and must be convinced that the U.S. does not seek to control Iraq oil.

The International Support Group should be organized to include all of the states bordering Iraq and vicinity. It is recommended that the Support Group work in conjunction and with the participation of the UN Secretary General.

An effort must be made to get both Iran and Syria to commit to constructive policies toward Iraq and furthermore stop the flow of equipment, technology and training of any groups resorting to violence in Iraq. Syria should help patrol its borders to the extent possible with patrols. It must be understood that no effort on our part will be successful without the active support and participation of each of the bordering nations and neighbors.

The Study Group recommends that the UN control and deal with Iran and its nuclear program. The Group clearly states that Iran and Syria must accept Israel's right to exist. It further suggests that Syria stop transporting shipments of weapons to the Hezbollah which supports the Palestinians.

Nations involved should consider some form of debt relief for Iraq. The cost is certainly justified to help establish peace.

In addition, I have taken the liberty to add the following: The United States should call for an international gathering of nations. The meeting must have the following nations present: Iraq, Iran, Syria, Israel, Turkey Saudi Arabia, Egypt, Pakistan, Afghanistan, Lebanon, Jordan, Oman, Kuwait, Russia, France, England, Japan, North and South Korea, Latvia, Lithuania, Norway, Sweden, Finland, Poland, the Czech Republic, the Ukraine and China. Each nation should be represented by responsible individuals, each with a full authority to make decisions. This would include, in several instances, the presence of religious leaders as well as political.

We need to discuss ways and means to "live and let live" – to build a better life for everyone – men, women and children, and improve each nation's economic welfare – lofty goals indeed but necessary to avoid unthinkable disaster if we continue on our present course. It must be understood that this is not a meeting to negotiate differences but rather to deliberate the consequences of failure to reach a fair and equitable solution.

In dealing with these nations, it is important to note we must not waste time in unproductive rhetoric. We cannot waste time on negotiations with radical nations who will not bend one iota in their distorted philosophy and who refuse to deviate from their convictions, right or wrong, i.e., recognizing Israel's request to exist, etc.

We need to reach the leaders of the world (global) community in which we live. Revenues from oil reserves and oil production must be carefully controlled and secured by meters to establish a fair and equitable means of distribution. There were other recommendations but all of the recommendations made by the study group should be given serious consideration. Your writer's personal views follow, which of course, just represent one man's opinion. My views are idealistic but then again, in my opinion, not any more idealistic than those of the study group.

Terrorists and insurgents alike will do everything and anything to disrupt any peace plan – any plan which run contrary to the radical philosophy. Thus it is imperative to have the full cooperation of all nations.

We need to ask them, to beseech them, to at least attempt to set aside their differences and historic rivalries. We must drop the non-productive political rhetoric currently in use and replace it with an honest effort to resolve our common global crisis in a realistic coalition of nations.

In that our global community will no longer permit isolation, we are dependent upon each other. We can reap the benefits of pooling our resources, to improve the standard of living for all mankind; i.e., hostilities, starvation, disease, etc., etc. Even our current oil crises have become an evil political disease, which must be dealt with more harmoniously – all nations working together can accomplish this.

Since its inception in 1945, the UN has failed to deliver its purported mandate. It has been unable to stop communist aggression in Korea. The U.S. had to undertake the task at considerable cost.

The UN's flaws are many, a cumbersome ponderous bureaucracy that has let thousands of people die in Africa, Asia and the Balkans, before it would act in their defense – if it did indeed act at all.

The UN has failed to stop slaughter in the Sudan. While thousands of people are dying from starvation and thousands more have been enslaved, raped and murdered, the UN has failed miserably to act. Any of the 135 states that are Signatories to the 1948 convention could have demanded international intervention. The U.S. Congress labeled it "genocide"!

The UN's halfhearted warnings and threats of calling for sanctions have proved meaningless. It involved the oil industry of Sudan. So, here again, national self-interests took precedence over a humanitarian problem.

The atrocities committed by Saddam Hussein and the potential threats which embodied his philosophy were not sufficient enough to compel any UN action. A real coalition of nations unfettered by national self-interest, i.e., oil, etc. – was beyond the political chicanery and debauchery of the ruling members.

The UN itself, particularly the Security Council, must be reformed, revamped and expanded. The permanent veto wielding council of only five members should be expanded to include eleven members – the only reason – this was actually difficult was due to historic rivalry and political difference. Let's open the proverbial door – it's about time to recognize the significance of more than five nations! Eleven nations would represent a far more equitable consensus.

The UN Charter needs to be ratified to provide a permanent Police Force consisting of a coalition of representative nations with the power and authority to use armed forces when necessary to accomplish its end. A UN Legislature should be provided. Here again, it's a global effort to maintain peace. It is not to be a global government – all provisions of the original UN Charter granting each member nation its right to form its own national government and national laws. However, it must clearly mandate that no nation has a right to impose by force its philosophy upon another nation and likewise, it must clearly mandate human rights. Each nation should have the right to follow its own culture, its own philosophy of life, etc. But NO nation should be permitted, much less encouraged, to distort history and foster the philosophy of hatred and killing and prejudice, but must give due respect to the customs and traditions of each culture and nation.

In about 1960 an incoming flood of ex-colonial nations seized control of the General Assembly of the UN. They then began to use the UN as a bargaining tool to extract concessions – selling favors to one another in the competition. America's power to defend its (the UN's) purpose was mitigated under the leadership of a couple of nations other than the U.S. Obviously that cannot be tolerated for the UN to function effectively.

All of this may appear idealistic… so let us be realistic and demand the impossible! We need to reconsider who we are and what we do, and how we do impacts others in our community of nations.

We rely on debate, discussion and dissent to determine our best course of action – dissent helped to shape America. But this must now be a truly cohesive effort involving all nations. The existing United Nations does not qualify under its current operational structure to satisfy the enforcement of common goals and shared values and interests of all nations.

The United Nations was formed shortly after World War II with the very best intentions to ensure that World War II would be the war to end all wars. Like the League of Nations this august body offered much hope to the world – which it failed to deliver!

One of the fundamental problems in the Middle East is the plight of the people who call themselves Palestinians and or refugees.

If peace is to prevail, then let's act boldly and let the truth be known. Let's clarify some of the myths – numerous articles and commentaries have appeared and facts documented and yet the myths remain.

Israel was created out of the Ottoman Empire at the end of World War I. Its legitimacy arises from the "Balfour Declaration", issued by the British who were given the mandate over the area by the League of Nations. Israel was to become the Jewish National Homeland. Of course, Jews have lived in the area since Biblical times.

In 1947, the British resigned their mandate and the UN partitioned the territory. The Arabs rejected the partition and launched a war against the Jews (Israel). War made refugees of many thousands despite the fact that the Jews offered to live in peace with them if they remained. However, they left the area hoping to return after the war. But the Israeli's defeated the Arabs against all odds winning a victory which astounded the world given the minute size of Israel. The war also left Israel in control of the West Bank and the Gaza Strip. Thus, the refugee problem had its inception. Today's refugees are, of course, generations apart from the original refugees.

Actually until 1948, the Jews in the region were known as the Palestinians. Palestinians are not a distinct nationality. The Arabs who call themselves Palestinians are no different than other Arabs who live in Syria, Jordan, Saudi or elsewhere. They came back to the area attracted to the success of those Jewish settlements in what was virtually wasteland. It is important to note that there were, obviously, some exceptions.

Later, the Oslo Accord, which was an attempt at peace, fell apart due to the actions of the now deceased Yassar Arafat.

According to the UN General Assembly in 1947, Jerusalem was to become an international city. Many Arabs contend that Jerusalem is their capital but the "infidel Jews" are in control of it. That of course is also a myth. Actually Jerusalem was never an Arab capital. Jerusalem is mentioned many times in the Jewish Bible, and it has been the center of the Jewish faith since the time of the Romans, who destroyed the Jewish Temple. Contrary to this, Jerusalem is not even mentioned in the Koran to my knowledge.

The Arabs, who appear to live in peace and harmony with the Jews of the city, now predominantly occupy East Jerusalem.

Israel has sacrificed vast areas to those calling themselves Palestinians to enable them to set up homes and live in peace. But these efforts on the part of Israel always seem to backfire. The Palestinians simply refuse to live in peace rejecting the right of the Jews to even exist. Arab children are taught to hate the Jews and some are not even aware of the existence of Israel. This has been going on now for almost 60 years.

The Arabs could resolve this festering sore but it seems as though they prefer to leave the situation as is because of their seething hatred toward Israel.

Sooner or later we must come to realize that we, the parents of children, are responsible for the hatred and prejudice which prevails. This is particularly true in the Mid-East where this hatred is deeply entrenched. The parents, the leaders and the teachers of the children are the root cause of the problem.

It is important to note that the "proper" education of children is the key factor here. They must be taught right from wrong and what is presented, as historical fact must not be distorted untruths. They must not be taught to hate and to kill and that others who may not agree with them are inferior. They must be taught that children of a different color or children who simply follow a different road to reach their God are not infidels deserving of death. Those who call themselves Palestinians today must be enlightened with historical fact. Jews were the "original Palestinians" and that Jews were living in the Holy land long before the birth of Christ. They are not intruders. Arab children must be taught that they can share a common ground and live in peace. It is only a question of changing the distorted views currently being promulgated.

It stands to reason that we are not going to reach the proselytizers of radical, hard-line Muslim philosophy and those who celebrate the hateful vision of Osama Ben Laden and others. Somehow, as difficult as it may be, we are going to have to re-education this radical element. In either case, we must mandate the education of minors (children and young adults) "devoid of hatred", killing and prejudice.

"Once upon a time", as grandma used to say… there were four very small children living in a very poor orphanage somewhere in a remote corner of our world. Jacob was a Jewish boy from Israel… Ali was a Muslim boy from Iraq… James was a Catholic boy from Ireland and Che was an Oriental boy from Peking, China. No child was over two years old when they were brought to the orphanage.

The folks at the orphanage, the caretakers, were a caring and kindly lot with lots of love to bestow on each of the children without any partiality. The children were really quite normal and reasonably healthy. From the beginning, they had to share their toys, clothing and food. They were encouraged and tutored to follow the traditional customs, religious practices and general ways attributed to their heritage. They were taught right from wrong and to respect the rights and feelings of their friends.

They just became the best of friends. In fact, they were inseparable and no one dared to come between them. As time went on the children became adults but remained as though they were blood brothers as long as they lived.

The moral of this simple story is obvious. These children were never taught to hate, never taught to discriminate because of a personal color or religious belief. They were virtually blind to discrimination and never understood how and why others throughout the world were discriminating.

Someone once said that most children are, at birth, open to all the impressions placed upon them and then became a product of those impressions – good, bad or indifferent. They are as a piece of soft clay, molded and formed to become what the artist's hands choose to make of it.

Unfortunately, too many parents cannot seem to understand this and, so, whatever prejudice exists in the parent, is given to the child. As discussed previously, there are countless thousands of Muslim children taught from birth to hate and kill and even to become martyrs in what they are told is a just cause.

Oddly enough there are only too many people who claim not to be prejudice – yet they think nothing of using expressions such as, "Oh that couple across the street, they're Jews" or "Oh, we just hired a Negro or a black man" or "Oh, our daughter's now going out with that Mexican (or Cuban or Jap) – innocent expressions, but what would be wrong with simply referring to the person by name or as a tall boy or a good looking girl or what have you but not by their color or racial heritage or religious preference!

Talk about impressions; consider the environment of a typical teenager today. Electronic computer games of terror, corruption, killing and crime personified. In the movies it is no different and it is appalling when we see small children taken to see some of these films. To say nothing of the impact of the drug dealers, it is tough for a kid today to cope with this pressure from some of his or her peers. This is the world we live in – we can do something about it but it is a real challenge.

In an article in Reader's Digest by Peter G. Peterson, dated October 2004, a theologian by the name of Dietrich Bonhoeffer was quoted as writing, "The ultimate test of a moral society is the kind of world that it leaves its children." We are failing that moral test!

It is important to re-emphasize that the "proper" education of children is the key factor here. They must be taught right from wrong and historical fact – not distorted untruths as described previously.

Those who call themselves Palestinians today must be enlightened with historical fact. That Jews were the "original Palestinians" and that Jews were living in the Holy

Land long before the birth of Christ. They are not intruders – it is their homeland also.

We are like a truck, on a highway without brakes – an accident about to happen. We are on a dangerous road and if we do not fix the brakes and resolve the problem at its source… i.e. the children… we are courting disaster.

As a nation, we are often accused of meddling in the affairs of other nations. Generally we become involved in assisting other nations in times of peril and disaster where help and aid are needed. However, with Iraq, we attempted to inculcate democracy as well. We have been accused of inciting other nations to seek nuclear weapons to defend themselves. We've been accused of overstepping our national borders in every way and have been harshly criticized for it.

Perhaps our interest and concern is due in part to our heritage. Our forefathers came here to escape tyranny and persecution and seek freedom. They have impressed us with their plight for freedom from oppression. So we, as free

Americans, tend to see freedom for others, wherever, whenever, we can as an inalienable right.

So many nations are still suffering under the rule of dictators, tyrants who suppress freedom of speech and religion and the right to a fair trial. These despots commit crimes against humanity with impunity. They become virtual butchers who rule with an iron hand. Such as the ruler in Sudan, I believe it is al-Bashir, who was responsible for killing over 200,000 people and over five million driven from their homes.

It is for this reason that I propose an appeal to humanity. Certainly we cannot remove all of these dictators from power. We cannot, overnight, change the world. We cannot even exert our influence in Iraq or Iran without being criticized. So, our only recourse is our appeal to humanity. If it's idealistic – so be it. But it's worth considering in an effort to prevent total disaster in one form or another.

"Until the philosophy which holds one race superior and another inferior is finally and permanently discredited and abandoned, everywhere is war… and until there is no longer first class and second class citizen of any nation, until the color of man's skin is of no more significance than the color of his eyes, and until the basic human rights are equally guaranteed to all without regard to race, there is war. And until that day the dreams of lasting peace, world citizenship, and rule of international morality will remain but a fleeting illusion, to be pursued, but never attained... now everywhere there is war." [Bob Marley (1945-1981) Jamaican Reggie musician. "War" (Song) on the album Rastaman Vibration Bob Marley and the Wailers (1976) the words of the song are based on a speech given to the United Nations by the Ethiopian Emperor Haile Selassit in 1968.]

PART III
THE IMMIGRATION ISSUE

The Immigration Crisis

This great nation of ours was founded by immigrants. Originally, we all came from somewhere else. We are a nation of immigrants and, together with the Native Americans (the American Indians) of this land we have all become the root of our heritage and the secret of our strength in this country.

We have, since our beginning, been a beacon to the people of other nations seeking freedom and opportunity. We draw power from this diversity.

Our attitudes have, however, been undergoing change in recent years. Our new immigrants are no longer welcomed with open arms, but rather viewed negatively as a possible liability or a form of charity. We now wonder whether or not we can afford to extend the proverbial "welcome mat", as we once did.

Immigrants arriving to this country at the beginning of this century were mostly of white (Anglo) European descent. However, during the 18th-19th centuries, due primarily to the slave trade, we had a great influx of black people of African descent arrive. After many years of trials and tribulations and unbearable prejudice, these people became citizens of this country.

Of course we have also opened our doors to vast numbers of immigrants from China, India, Mexico and other countries.

During the latter part of the 20th century and now in the 21st century we have experienced a large influx of immigrants from Mexico and Cuba. While many of these residents have come here in earnest, passing through our customs with legal passports and following all the rules and procedures applied to a legal entry into this country... too many have not!

We can now account for illegal immigrants entering this country and managing to remain here, without going through our "due process" as applied to immigration, amounting to numbers reaching into the millions. Mexicans share of the total unauthorized resident population increased from 58% in 1990 to 69% in 2000 alone. In addition to Mexico, six countries had more than 100,000 unauthorized residents in the United States in January 2000: El Salvador, Guatemala, Columbia, Honduras, China and Ecuador. This has caused concern involving racial, ethnic, cultural, political and economic issues.

Together with the surge of legal immigrants coming to us from neighboring border nations, we are experiencing an inordinate number of people crossing our borders illegally.

Like other issues representing a challenge and seeking resolution, such as our health care system, energy and terrorism, the United States immigration policy has reached crisis status demanding our full attention and some resolution.

In January 2004, President Bush introduced a "Guest Worker" idea in an effort to woo Hispanic populations in Arizona, New Mexico and Florida. The President's proposal would allow the roughly eight million illegal aliens in the United States to apply for temporary work permits, good for three years. These permits could then be renewed at least once.

The proposal was not met favorably, creating a lot of criticism. The INS estimates that the total unauthorized immigration population residing in the U.S. in January 2000 was 7 million. Population grew by about 350,000 per year from 1990-1999. Total all immigrants immigrating from 1981-1996 from all countries was 13,484,275. Mexico is the largest source for unauthorized immigration into the United States.

The Immigration and Naturalization Service (INS) estimates of unauthorized immigrants refer to foreign born persons who entered without inspection or who violated the terms of a temporary admission and who have not acquired proper legal status or gained temporary protection against removal by applying for an immigration benefit.

Unfortunately, most of us have not given a great deal of thought to the impact these immigrants, particularly the illegal ones, have on our way of life and how they are affecting our society. The illegal immigrants have become a heavy burden on our health care system, our education system, our security system and our water and food supply.

An estimated 6 million illegal aliens work in our economy, yet no taxes are received from either the employer or the employee.   The practice of paying "cash wages" by employers who have hired these illegal immigrants deprives the U.S. Government of many millions of dollars in employment taxes.

The following graph shows that even though the U.S. had started to achieve a stable population in 1970, mass immigration is driving our population ever upwards.

U.S. Population and Immigration Data, Projections and Graphs

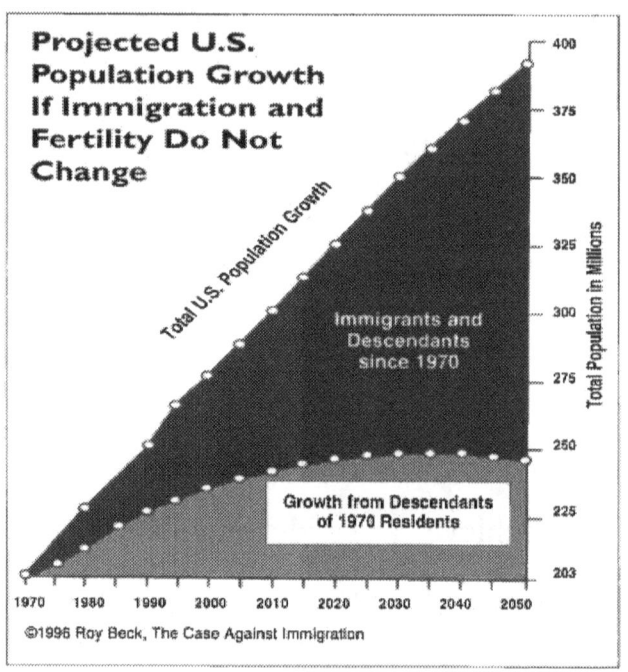

Projected U.S. Population Growth If Immigration and Fertility Do Not Change

Total U.S. Population Growth

Immigrants and Descendants since 1970

Growth from Descendants of 1970 Residents

Total Population in Millions

400 · 375 · 350 · 325 · 300 · 275 · 250 · 225 · 203

1970 1980 1990 2000 2010 2020 2030 2040 2050

©1996 Roy Beck, The Case Against Immigration

Sources: US Census Bureau;
demographer Leon Bouvier;
Roy Beck, <u>Numbers USA</u>

The top line of the above graph shows actual US population from 1970 to 1993, and the US Census Bureau "medium projection" of total population size from 1994 to 2050. It assumes fertility, mortality, and mass immigration levels will remain similar to 1993. In fact, overall immigration has continued to rise significantly, meaning that population growth will actually be higher than shown here.

The lower portion of the graph represents growth from 1970 Americans and their descendants. There were 203 million people living in the US in 1970. The projection of growth in 1970-stock

112

Americans and their descendants from 1994 to 2050 is based on recent native-born fertility and mortality rates. This growth would occur despite below replacement-level fertility rates because of population momentum, where current and future children of the current generation will grow up to have their own children, all during the lifetime of the current generation. Nevertheless, this segment of Americans is on track to peak at 247 million in 2030 and then gradually decline.

The upper portion of the graph represents the difference between the number of 1970-stock Americans and the total population. The tens of millions of people represented by this block are the immigrants who have arrived, or are projected to arrive, since 1970, plus their descendents, minus deaths. They are projected to comprise 90% of all US population growth between 1993 and 2050.

See the NumbersUSA website at www.numbersusa.com for a more thorough and interesting presentation of these facts - view the topics presented on the right side of the page.

The following table shows how the current level of mass immigration vastly exceeds traditional levels.

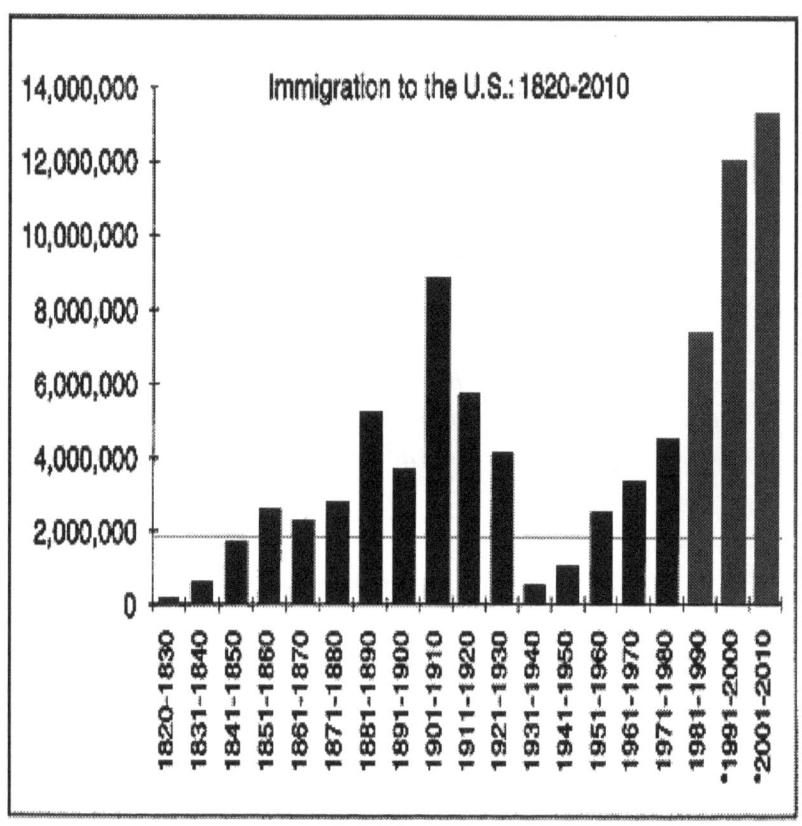

Projections and graph courtesy Population Environment Balance,
email uspop at balance dot org
Sources: US Census Bureau; Statistical Yearbook,
Immigration and Naturalization Service
Averages: 178,000 per year from 1925-1965,
195,000 per year from 1921-1970

History shows the U.S. has traditionally allowed relatively small numbers to immigrate, thus allowing for decades of assimilation. After the peak of about 8.7 million in the first decade of the 20th century, numbers went steadily down. Immigration averaged only 178,000 per year from 1925 through 1965!

Federal agents, along with local authorities, have been conducting background checks on prison inmates in an attempt to identify illegal immigrants. The resulting statistics are alarming. The border patrol's Yuma Sector saw a staggering 54% jump in arrests in fiscal year 2005.

Smuggling humans into our country has become a very large and profitable trade, not to mention, the dealers in drug trafficking. Most frightening, of course, are the terrorists who also find ways to pass through our borders unchecked! About half of the nearly 190,000 illegal immigrants deported in 2006 had criminal records, according to U.S. authorities.

People from Central America are attempting to make their way here. Every few days 3-500 of them attempt to make their way to the U.S. through rugged terrain and facing

Mexican corrupt "hoods" out to make an illegal buck. It's a very dangerous journey but like others, they are determined to seek a better way of life.

Our Department of Homeland Security is likewise faced with trying to share the burden of border control but, like their peers the border patrol, their efforts are seemingly fruitless… they keep coming!

This unchecked immigration problem of illegal aliens from our Latin neighbors to the south of us can no longer be deferred as a racial problem, but rather needs to be seen as an economic, social and military problem. Of course, pushing for immigration reform is particularly difficult in a nation so divided politically.

The contemplated 700-mile border fence could conceivably provide some restraint but it is doubtful it would resolve the problem. Sophisticated electronic surveillance will certainly offer some help to deter the illegal aliens. An investment in additional border patrol, special agents, while costly, will also help. Special teams of highly trained and armed "border militia" might serve to discourage these large and armed border smugglers.

It is, of course, a problem not easily dealt with. As for example, the tunnels which gangs of racketeers manage to dig out along our borders opening the way for illegal traffic of one form or another. Only too often, there are corrupt people on one side or the other behind these bold criminal activities.

The laws currently on the books provide large fines for employers who hire illegal immigrants; however, these laws are not enforced. Out of compassion we provide social programs including costly medical treatment for these people. It becomes charity and is considered extremely costly.

Another problem is the uninsured driver with very poor driving habits. Unfortunately, this applies to the vast majority of illegal immigrants.

Every effort is and has been made to solicit the cooperation of Mexico. We are aware that they harbor many corrupt officials but we cannot seem to convince higher levels of their government to act on this. Our relations with the Mexican government appear to be good but we are not able to pierce this self-righteous armor they wear.

President Bush recently toured Brazil, Uruguay, Columbia, Guantomino and Mexico. The United States immigration policies were paramount in discussions. We have been criticized for being too harsh on immigration with particular reference to "the fence project" along our border.

President Bush wants to establish his guest worker program and a path to citizenship for many of the 12 million undocumented immigrants we harbor.

Backers of overhauling our immigration rules are attempting to give legal status to the 1.5 illegal immigrants working, which would provide a labor pool for U.S. agriculture. Of course 80-85% of these immigrants from Mexico lack legal documentation.

The estimated combined annual gross income of all U.S. workers born in Latin American of both legal and illegal immigration status according to a 2004 report was roughly $450 billion, although 93% of that was spent in the U.S.

It is estimated that above 6.3 million illegal immigrants were living in the U.S. in 2005.

The Mexican government contends that poor living conditions contribute to these poor Mexican families seeking a better life. However, nothing is said about the Mexican police and the Mexican military and only too many government officials of Mexico who are corrupt and are largely responsible.

The INS identified five ways in which unauthorized residents can leave the unauthorized resident population each year. They can: (1) be removed by the INS, (2) die, (3) emigrate, (4) adjust to a lawful status in the United States or (5) depart briefly from the US and return with immigrant visas allowing them to reside here legally.

There is no international obligation for any nation to allow others to enter or to work or to permanently settle within its geographical borders.

If we take a very liberal stand imposing fewer restrictions, we have, essentially defeated our purpose. If we increase restrictions imposing more rigorous restraints on immigrants, then we encourage and magnify the problem of illegal immigration.

Should we continue to allow a free flow of immigrants to this country? Or should we tighten our belt and make it increasingly more difficult to immigrate to this country? It appears as a case of "you can't win for losing" – either way we lose.

About two-thirds of all U.S. citizens recognize this problem as a crisis. They understand the economics – that providing free social services to illegal aliens is costly. They also understand that these same illegal aliens contribute to an increased crime rate. These same people agree that something must be done about it.

In either case, it is apparent we must continue to employ every means possible to secure our borders from illegal entry. This is true, if for no other reason than that of the flow of illegal drug traffic and the threat that illegal terrorists place upon us.

Border intelligence must be increased to break down these established illegal groups, gangs – they are well organized and in most instances, well armed. They present a serious threat to us. For example, smuggling of human traffic, drug smuggling and terrorists!

Our border patrol should have an elite special task force, specially trained and armed to the teeth, with approval to use their weapons where necessary – similar to local police SWAT teams.

If these illegals are caught they must not be released so easily – simply due to a lack of space. It may be more economical for us to build temporary prisons to detain these individuals until they can be deported rather than sustain and absorb the cost of freeing them to do more costly damage.

The guest worker program is practical, providing every worker is given a complete "check up" and ID card before going to work.

Another program had been proposed relating to our existing illegal alien situation, along the lines of providing an opportunity for them to become citizens if they have been here over two years. If not, a special program should be worked out to penalize, but not unfairly, to provide motivation for them to acquire proper ID.

In all cases, however, a system should be worked out to make it possible for these illegal folks to contribute to the social benefits they receive, based upon their income without working an undue hardship. But social service should be provided to them through a special program, whereby they contribute something – it's not a "freebee"!

Technology and our vast resources have provided well for us thus far. However, increased population growth without reasonable and adequate measures to keep it under control could present a serious threat to our ecological system.

PART IV
OUR HEALTH CARE DILEMMA

Our Health Care Crisis – An Introduction

In our global community, we are currently preeminent in power and in wealth. Our vast natural resources, our impressive technological production capabilities and our comparatively well-educated population are the envy of our global neighbors.

The medical industry has been both innovative and prolific in developing patient diagnostic and treatment technology. This new medical technology is able to perform wonders for man, offering to improve his physical and mental well being and longevity – progress is costly... costs are skyrocketing and our ability to cope with these revolutionary innovations and costs is a challenge which we have not had much success with. Despite much success with medical progress, we are not, by any means, the healthiest nation in the country, nor do we have an effective health care delivery system – certainly not one able to deal with the onslaught of the formidable and complex, intractable, medically-related issues facing our nation today.

"Every American must have access to all the benefits modern medicine can provide."[13] Physicians are entitled to be adequately compensated for their costly education and dedication. Pharmacy manufacturers are likewise entitled to just compensation for costly research and to reasonable profit. The same applies to those who have developed new medical equipment, diagnostic and surgical treatment instruments and tests. Each is entitled to a fair return.

Our Troubled Health Care System

Our Medicare and Medicaid systems are both in trouble. Government cutbacks in physician reimbursements have caused the physicians to rebel and threaten to drop Medicare patients and not take any new patients. State governments are also burdened with deficits, reducing their approved services for the less well to do. Recently, high health care costs have been referred to as "Health Inflationitis".

Insurance companies have increased their premiums, employers have had to pass these increases on to employees and they provide fewer benefits to reduce the cost further. "Today, 44 million people in the U.S. have no health insurance. Eight out of ten of them are unemployed or are dependent. On a national basis annual health care expenditures per capita have increased from $1,067 in 1980 to $6,135 today. The crisis is expected to continue to increase to $10,000 by 2012."[14] Too many Americans have little or no access to medical care. A large number of retirees too young to qualify for coverage under Medicare must insure themselves. Only a few years ago health maintenance organizations (HMOs) had been relatively effective in pushing down premiums. However, premiums are again rising only too quickly, while benefits are cut back.

Administrative costs for pencil pushing throughout the medical industry are astronomical, ineffective and unnecessary, especially with the electronic technology available today. Many thousands of dollars are lost in the process of filing medical claims manually. They are time consuming and invite only too many errors. These claims are returned for additional information but many just sit in a drawer in the doctor's office.

Those lost dollars in revenue are taken up by doctors charging more. Another nasty and costly item resulting from many of these manual claims is fraudulent medical diagnostic treatment coding, adding up to millions each year nationally. "For every hour of patient care, 30 minutes of paper work is generally required."[15]

Tens of thousands die from medical errors each year and many more are injured. Our immigration policies are not effective and virtually uncontrolled. Immigration year after year is placing a strain on our social resources. It has been said that some crime syndicates have established medical clinics to launder their money. That situation represents a sizable piece of change too.

In 1980 half of all workers were over age 65. Today 62% or more are – that means bigger doctor bills. In 1996 the Employee Benefit Research Institute found that the typical under-35 male worker had about $750 in medical costs a year. But more spending on the 35-49 year old males jumped to $1,200 (as of 2001) and expenses rise faster in workers close to retirement. Political interference into health care, while protecting patients, also adds to costs. I.e.: patient rights etc.

Baby boomers are coming of age and "80% of them plan to work during their retirement."[16] We are living longer. Life expectancy increased in this last century from 50 to almost 80 for women and to 74 for men.

Discoveries in genetics and immunology will make it possible to slow the aging process itself, increasing life expectancy. Future projections call for the amount of

Americans over 65 to increase traumatically. As a result, programs designed for senior citizens could comprise a very substantial percentage of the federal budget. "77.2 years is the average life expectancy of an American child born today?"[17] "It becomes readily apparent, therefore, that in the not too distant future... the elderly will become the dominant force in the United States. Thus, by 2033 more than one of every five Americans will be elderly."[18]

Commentary on the Causations of Our Health Care Crisis

Each of the problems in the health care crisis compendium just covered is a great concern to Americans. Each demands some form of resolution. However, there is no "magic elixir" potion, no "universal band-aid" to apply which will resolve all the problems. It is important that we focus first on the entire dilemma from a more philosophical viewpoint rather than treat each problem separate from the others – for they are related and they do interact.

What is called for is a radical change in our philosophical approach. Our present system is focused on acute episodic care. It is a system predicated upon curing the ill as opposed to preventing illness. For example, a change from an illness-based system to one based upon wellness.

To accomplish this requires a concentration, alertness if you will, to impending ailments in the offing and an effort to do what we can to prevent the illness from occurring. It is a case of preventative medicine versus the pill, surgery, caster oil and the band-aid.

According to the centers for disease control and prevention (CDS) conditions such as heart disease, cancer, high blood pressure, diabetes and asthma are now the leading causes of illness, disability and death in the United States. They account for seven out of every ten deaths and affect the quality of life of 90 million Americans.

"66% of American adults are seriously overweight or obese."[19] "400,000 Americans will die this year from obesity-related causes and in the next few years, obesity will replace tobacco as the leading cause of preventable death."[20]

We could cut the cost of diabetes by 50% if we did early screening. We need to start teaching children nutrition and to look at obesity problems.

Discoveries in genetics and immunology will make it possible to slow the aging process itself and increase life expectancy.

Future projections call for Americans over 65 to increase dramatically. As a result, programs need to be designed to accommodate senior citizens, which will comprise a substantial percentage of income in the federal budget. A more vigorous elderly population will transform America, once youth oriented, into a mature society.

In a recent article appearing in the Star Banner (Ocala, Florida), Wednesday, July 28th 2004, Tommy G. Thompson, the Secretary of Health and Human Services said, "Medicare had it backwards, spending 99% of its resources treating seniors after they got sick and only 1% on preventing illness and promoting wellness." Hopefully, new Medicare laws have changed this approach.

Medicare currently covers a wide variety of preventive services (i.e. tests, etc.) However, the new Medicare bill will expand preventive coverage... i.e. free initial comprehensive physicals for new beneficiaries and screening tests for cholesterol and diabetes, tests for people already in this program.

Adults over the age of 40 are prone to develop multiple problems such as high blood pressure, overweight conditions, insulin resistance and abnormal cholesterol and triglyceride levels – placing them at risk for diabetes and on the fast track to coronary artery disease. Overweight or obese children are also at risk for developing diabetes and this is fast becoming another crisis.

By the year 2030, almost 20% of the United States will be 65 and older. This presents a formidable challenge to our health care system.

Medicare fraud, corruption and abuse have threatened the very fiber of the system. The state of Texas recovered over $74 million in one year from fraud!

Our emergency rooms are overcrowded throughout the nation – filled to capacity with a critical shortage of "ER" doctors and nurses.

Illegal immigrants are running up costs. In only too many instances they are provided with few medical benefits including hospital care, medication and costly diagnostic tests – at no cost to them – free!

Counterfeit drugs are finding their way into the hands of trusting consumers. Empty gelatin capsules are filled with worthless powder and labeled with phony labels. The statistics are astounding.

Physicians will often attempt to maximize their service, wherever and whenever possible by miscoding the medical codes used in their claims. One small variation can and often does lead to a lot of additional revenue. For example, a simple return visit to check on a patient – a visit less than five minutes coded as a full physical examination – and no one is the wiser!

Our present health care system has a tendency to penalize people who do have health care coverage through their employer.

The High Cost of Drugs

Recent reports would indicate that the American consumer is charged the highest price for prescription drugs in the world.

According to Peter Rost, M.D., Vice President of Marketing, for the Endocrinology Division of Pfizer, Inc., more than 700,000 Americans die each year from heart disease. He refers to studies showing that 50% of people on cholesterol-lowering drugs don't use them as prescribed, and the more they have to pay, the more they stop taking them. "So it is obvious that probably tens of thousands of Americans are dying because they can't afford drugs."

Reports of numerous incidents of people who, because they cannot afford the high cost of their drugs, have simply cut the drug dose in half or even in quarters, figuring some is better than none – thus not following the prescription and endangering their condition.

A United States Congressional study concluded, "On the average brand name drug prices charged by manufacturers wholesalers and retailers were higher in the United States by about 70%. "It's an outrage what is going on," says Senator Byron Dorean.

We pay 60% more than the British or the Swiss for the same drugs according to testimony before the Senate Committee on Government Affairs, and two-thirds more than the Canadians.

Once admired, the pharmaceutical industry may have lost its ethical way, become more concerned with protecting its bottom line, than with the patient's health.

Two in three Americans now believe that drug prices are unreasonably high and 60% favor federal price controls as a solution, according to the latest poll.

When Dr. Peter Rost was asked to comment about the drug industries' constant argument that reduced American prices and government price controls would decimate the profits and destroy vital research, he responded, "It's just not true!"

Time Magazine recently quoted some statistics – "$2 billion, the amount pharmaceutical companies have agreed to pay the U.S. since 2001 to settle illegal sales and marketing practices." "93% increase in total spending on pharmaceutical promotion in the U.S. from 1997-2002."

The Federal Trade Commission (FTC) claims some pharmaceutical manufacturers also violate antitrust laws by agreeing to delay the introduction of a generic version of a new drug.

The drug industry has taken a firm stand on price change applying powerful influence in Washington with their overwhelming number of lobbyists. Congress has fallen prey to this pressure, passing laws favoring the drug industry's position.

High quality miracle drugs don't come cheaply in an era of onerous Food and Drug Administration to efficiency standards. However, once approved these same drugs cost very little to reproduce.

Big drug companies generally spend less on research and development than they make in profit – sometimes much less. They spend vast sums on promotion and advertising and big executive salaries – apparently without regard to the fact that some people just cannot afford their high prices and must do without.

It's interesting to note that much of the creative work in coming up with new drugs is usually done in universities and government labs – not in licensed industries.

Of all the drugs the FDA has approved over the past six years – fully 78% were classified as unlikely to be better than existing drugs and 60% didn't even contain new ingredients – so they were just old prescriptions in slightly different forms, called by the industry "me-too" drugs! In 2001 of the 78% approved, only seven were truly new and innovative.

Our government has warned drug makers about the industry's costly and often "questionable" marketing tactics such as perks for doctors that may be in violation of federal fraud and kickback laws and showering doctors with expensive meals, trips and other costly incentives to induce them to prescribe their products. This may appear reasonable on the surface but it is not only costly, it may also tend to influence a physician's judgment in prescribing one drug versus another, which may be even better for the patient.

Drug companies obviously have a contract with the Federal Government Veteran's Administration. The VA provides a program which enables most veterans to secure virtually any drug prescribed by the VA doctor upon examination (and/or by reference from another physician and then approved by the VA doctor) at a nominal $7 for a 30-day supply of the drug. Why then, won't the drug companies at least contract with Medicare to provide the same benefits for the Medicare patient?

Many large, foreign pharmaceutical manufacturers will sell their drugs to the U.S. at a very high price then turn around and sell the same product to other countries for a much lower price. The reasoning here is that the foreign countries receiving the lower cost have government price controls on their drugs.

The Bush Administration is reported as saying that importation would allow unsafe drugs into the country. It would expose Americans to greater potential risk of harm from unsafe or ineffective drugs, would be extremely costly to implement and would overwhelm the FDA is already heavily burdened and regulated system.

There are, of course, other ways of dealing with importation which would, quite possibly, make it more reliable and secure for the American public. But this does not address the crux of the drug price problem. It simply would apply a weak band-aid! Likewise, neither will the new Medicare drug discount card which didn't even begin until 2006. Oh, it has helped, but it is not a solution – just another band-aid!

What then can the American people (i.e. the government) do to provide some relief? AARP once advocated a "prescription drug affordability campaign" which has three major goals:

Goal 1: Legalize the importation of drugs from Canada and other countries. AARP is fighting to support bipartisan legislation that will legalize the importation of prescription drugs from other countries starting with Canada.

Goal 2: Empower our government to negotiate lower prices. AARP will then support legislation empowering our federal government to negotiate lower rates for Medicare beneficiaries.

Goal 3: Force the pharmaceutical industry to reform. Apply pressure on the industry to limit price increases to no more than the rate of inflation and require them to more prominently disclose information about their risks and effectiveness.

With regard to Goal 1, it is assumed that a prescription would be required to be ordered and that the order could only be placed with a foreign company, retailer, distributor or other type of entity which has first had full clearance and authorization from our government. On the surface, this alone would appear to be a formidable task and at a prohibitive cost. However, with the full cooperation of all parties concerned, it is not an impossible task. Here again, it is only a band-aid!

As more people take more drugs for more conditions, adverse reactions become a serious threat in themselves.

Experts believe that one in four nursing home admissions is drug related. One in five Americans over 65 has been improperly prescribed drugs, mainly barbiturates and tranquilizers, that can impair balance and cause fatigue and mental confusion as reported in the Federal Agency for Health Care Research and Quality, the December 12, 2001, issue of the journal of the American Medical Association.

Age related change in the way the body absorbs drugs and eliminates toxins sometimes means that older patients need lower doses. "It's vital for all of us to pay close attention to any symptoms that coincide with their taking a new drug," says Ellen Flaherty, coordinator of geriatric nurse practitioner training at New York University.

Most seniors don't have coordinated medical care and the pharmacist on your block doesn't normally know what the pharmacist on the other side of town is doing.

Adverse interactions are also possible in those who take over-the-counter drugs and herbal supplements along with prescribed drugs. A doctor should routinely review and compare these medications. Unfortunately, most physicians do not!

While a physician may scan briefly, a patient's record for medications currently being taken, the physician will neglect to consider over-the counter medications and/or vitamins, minerals and herbs. A specialist may have prescribed a medication which the patient is currently taking but not listed on the primary doctor's patient record, thus, the doctor would miss this. Now, if that doctor was prescribing a normally effective combination of medications for this patient – a serious negative interaction could occur.

Malpractice Insurance

The high cost of malpractice insurance is forcing many doctors out of the "high risk" specialties and others to maximize patient volume by cutting back on time spent with patients and charging whatever they can get away with, resorting in too many instances, in poor patient service.

In summation, Florida Blue Cross and Blue Shield in their "Florida Blue" publication sum up what is driving up health care costs very succinctly as follows:

- Litigation and Risk Management
- Rising Provider Expenses
- Government Mandates and Regulations
- Increased Consumer Demand
- General Inflation
- Drugs, Medical Devices and other Medical Advances

Drugs – Substance Abuse, Narcotics Trafficking

One of our nation's critical problems (crisis) is and has been substance abuse in alcohol, tobacco and narcotics. These abuses add to the fiscal burden and strain of our health care system and contribute to the ill health, disability and death of millions of Americans every year – and this is a preventable problem!

Whether it is the alcohol, tobacco or illicit drugs, their use can result in dire consequences to one's health, occupation, psychological well being and/or occupational functioning.

Genetics

The Challenge and Opportunity - Stem Cell Research

Stem cell research, cloning and genetic engineering have become the new frontiers of science. It is said that stem cell research holds immense promise for millions of Americans suffering from diseases like diabetes, Parkinson's, Alzheimer's and heart disease.

It is, however, a violation of the elementary notion that we don't make of the human embryo a thing, made and used as a mere instrument for others. Some people are saying that human embryos merit respect as a form of human life and federal dollars should not be used to encourage their destruction.

The dubious distinction between therapeutic cloning and reproductive cloning raises some imponderable questions – moral, legal and otherwise. It is a very complex controversial revolutionary medical issue.

Stem cells have spurned grand predictions and hot debates. Stem cell research offers hope for the cure of dreadful diseases where, heretofore, there was no hope. Researchers have been injecting stem cells into paralyzed rats and watching their spinal cords mend.

President Bush vetoed a bill that would have expanded funding for embryonic stem cell research. Meanwhile, patients with Parkinson's disease aren't sure how long they can hang on. The debate is politically motivated together with strong religious convictions.

The argument, simple enough, is that it is not right to destroy a human life in order to save another. Opponents contend that the destruction of embryos involved in research is immoral. Protagonists argue that a stem cell embryo doesn't count as a human life when compared with the life it could save.

Researchers are offering alternatives to the stem cell controversy by suggesting the use of amniotic fluid, which would "side step" the embryo controversy. Here again, success or failure is ponderable, but remains hopeful. Most doctors agree studies should continue.

This new frontier also presents risks. The FDA is concerned with patient safety. Another concern is how a stem cell is grown and the risks of contamination in the process. Likewise, we have concern over side effects. Another concern involves the actions of unscrupulous sorts who would go to any extreme or measure to profit from stem cells as a racket!

As this book is being written, stem cell research bills are being presented in Congress to overturn President Bush's vetoes.

Other nations are picking up the pace on their own but only time will tell whether success or failure will follow.

Application of "Practical" Medicine Today

Nutrition education is taught in medical schools. However, schools of public health have not historically placed any emphasis on the subject; certainly no concentration of the subject is promoted as a valuable support to a medical practice.

Doctors generally will refrain from prescribing a patient program designed to meet dietary requirements with supplementation. i.e. Vitamins, minerals and herbs – natural medicine! Yet, millions of Americans are turning to vitamins, herbs and other natural remedies. They are turning to alternative therapies for help even while using medications or other forms of conventional care.

One study showed that in a single year, two million hospital patients had serious adverse drug effects and about 100,000 died because of their conventional prescription drug treatment, making prescription drugs one of the top causes of death in this country." This is not meant to say that millions of lives are not also saved; however, the point here is that total dependence on prescription drugs as a panacea, a cure for all ailments by itself, exclusive of other considerations – needs to be carefully reconsidered.

Many drugs are dangerous especially when taken over long periods of time. Likewise, we often end up taking action to stop drug interactions – equally dangerous!

Often alternative cures are available – a program of a high dose of certain vitamins, minerals or herbs can often help to control systems of certain diseases without drugs.

The medical community is and has been reluctant to accept natural remedies. This is, of course, characteristic of medical practice – anything new – a new approach, a new program of treatment is generally accepted only after a long period of time. Most physicians actually shun suggestions of an alternative "natural" approach to medicine. One reason, of course, is that the pharmacy industry has quite literally brainwashed most physicians so they react accordingly. As a result the medical establishment largely ignores many of the natural therapies which could be beneficial.

Physicians should provide guidelines about how to safely use approved drugs along with alternative therapies in order to improve logical treatment regimens.

A note here is in order regarding the current vitamin and mineral industry. Like the pharmacy industry, it could stand considerable improvement and control. Simple and effective remedies have passed on from generation to generation. Herbs have been applied effectively for literally thousands of years and grandma's chicken soup is still, to this day, considered a good tonic for the common cold. People often don't realize how many remedies and healing herbs are as close as their kitchen and Mother Nature provides a prodigious cornucopia of natural health care remedies.

People are trying to avoid the high cost of using the health care system. Some are using homeopathic remedies as ways to treat viruses instead of antibiotics and risking developing a resistance. They are asking, "What can we do naturally?" In many cases herbs can both heal and nourish the body and keep it well.

The fact that so many people are eager to try supplements, particularly when it is hard to find reliable information about them, indicates that major changes in health care have brought herbal and nutritional remedies closer to mainstream medicine. Traditionally, the medical community has been skeptical of these remedies and of alternative medicine – but that is changing.

Most pharmaceutical manufacturers do not generally promote nutritional supplements (herbs, vitamins and minerals). Doctors do not receive new information about the nutritional value of these "natural" medications unless they go out of their way to study them. The vitamin, mineral and herb industry is, of course, totally unregulated – a few words of caution are in order…

Unfortunately, more often than not, the hype used to describe a product, needs to be examined carefully – what's advertised is not always what you get…. What's on the label is not necessarily supported by scientific evidence to support the purported value. Simply listing studies to bolster a claim is not adequate unless these are clinical studies accepted for publication in <u>Peer Review Journals</u> and that, as a rule, is simply not the case!

In a 1998 article in the AMA's Archives of Internal Medicine, Dr. James A. Goodwin and Dr. Michael R. Tangun, of the University of Texas, explored why medical school professors have been historically antagonistic toward complementary medicine. The authors concluded that medical professors resist the idea of vitamin therapy because it comes from a realm outside of medical schools. The authors also indicated that the financial incentives of patentable drugs drive pharmaceutical companies more so than vitamins.

Jeffrey Bland, PhD, President and Chief Science Officer of the White House Commission on Complementary and Alternative Medicine, agrees. In his March 27, 2001, address to the Commission, Bland said, "Historically, clinical nutrition and nutritional supplementation have not played a significant role in medical education. These topics have been excluded from medical school curricula since the university system was separated from land grant colleges or agricultural schools. Doctors, who were principally males, were trained at the university, while women and farmers went to agricultural colleges, where their subjects included nutrition, home economics, and dietetics. Male doctors came to regard nutrition as unscientific, or 'women's work.' This bias has characterized the role of nutritional supplements in medicine for the past 40 years."

An article appearing in the June/July 2004 issue of an Integrative Medicine Publication written by Dr. Charles R. Elder, entitled "Integrating Natural Medicine into conventional Clinic Practices," illustrates the subject clearly from a practitioner's vantage point.

It would appear that a growing number of primary care clinicians desire the integration of complementary and alternative medicine (CAM) into conventional clinic practices.

Based upon the Vedic (VM) paradigm, this system has been successfully implemented within the settling of a large established Health Maintenance Organization (HMO). The clinic curriculum introduces patients to fundamental principals of VM and provides prescriptions encompassing diet, daily routine, stress management, herb supplements and other culturally acceptable modalities. VM as a prevention oriented paradigm ideally complements the usual allopathic care.

Several conventional allopathic specialists enable the HMO clinicians to conveniently generate referrals on the organizations electronic menu by the same process used for conventional specialty consultations.

In other words, a patient arrives with a medical problem – is seen by a doctor or doctors, tests are administered, referrals are handled automatically in the same office – so a patient gets a thorough exam after which he or she is provided with a more valid diagnosis, prognoses and a full treatment regimen.

Patients react with an enhanced sense of control over their medical condition. The VM synthesizes and turns the Vedic science into a single consciousness based approach to treating illness and promoting health. In addition to improved patient satisfaction, a reduction of costs is an added advantage.

This kind of holistic care would not be possible within the time restraints of traditional one-on-one primary care visits and it produces a more secure interaction and better monitoring of a patient's condition.

Obviously, there are problems to be faced in the transition. However, these problems are not formidable ones and can be overcome without difficulty – but a radical change of this magnitude will not come about easily.

Consider by contrast, a typical patient visit. Most doctors are very busy – in fact rushed. Patients rarely are given time to really go over all the symptoms of what ails them. Invariably the doctor is interrupted during the consultation. The doctor generally prescribes a pill (the proverbial band-aid) and suggests that the patient return in a week or so, depending upon condition. Upon the patient's return, if the patient's condition has not improved, another pill prescription is provided or the patient is referred for additional diagnostic tests or sent to a specialist for further consultation or any combination of the others. The specialist may run additional tests and then prescribe different medications, etc.

The patient, in the interim is confused, concerned and upset. Perhaps the patient is taking over the counter medications and/or herbal supplements – the doctor is generally not interested in that (with exception) there could very well be other problems in the patient's condition which have not been considered or drug interactions etc. Any number of undiagnosed conditions could be responsible if the patient has been given the "rush job" – unable to tell it all!

While this may appear overly dramatic and exaggerated – it is only too often very typical – not atypical!

Medical Administration

Today's physicians are overwhelmed with a crushing burden of bureaucracy and patient load. It is a challenge to keep pace with the sheer volume of new medical information.

Back when medical claims were processed manually by physicians, clinics and hospitals – medical billing was considered a nightmare. Public and private such as Medicare, Medicaid, Champus, VA, commercial insurance carriers each required a different claim form.

These were the dark ages of medical data processing. Today medical claims are codified (universal). All hospitals use one form, all physicians another and dentists another etc. Yet we still have not managed to bring medical data processing into the 21st century. We need to use "state of the art" information systems and technology more efficiently to more effectively deliver medical services.

Electronic claims processing is available and reasonable. Medical data such as a patient's diagnosis, cure, and treatments and procedures codes together with other pertinent data, all are systemically keyed into the physicians and/or the hospitals computer system.

It goes from there, electronically, to a central clearing (audit) house. The data is checked for omissions, errors, duplications and so forth. From there it is again sent electronically, this time to the insurance carrier for payment. This procedure reduces serious errors substantially. It reduces payment turn around time and increases cash flow.

It is also interesting to note that this same system may be amplified and used even more effectively to control overcharges and improper charges once a patient's initial "basic data" is entered: i.e., patient's condition, diagnosis and the prescriptions and treatments and/or other medical devices prescribed and, in the case of a physician, the nature of the visit or return visit, and, in the case of a hospital, the length of stay. The clearinghouse system can then analyze this data on a comparative basis to see if what is being done is what would normally be done given the same medical data. Compared by hospital, by physicians, and possibly even by geographical data, i.e. different circumstances attributed to different areas.

This kind of data analysis would call attention and possibly alleviate many of the problems we currently experience – certainly in medical billing.

As a case in point... currently, "the private companies that process claims for Medicare made nearly $20 billion in erroneous or questionable payments in 2003, an error rate of 93%."[21]

"The innocuous prescription pad – it is antiquated, inefficient and dangerous, killing patients and driving up health care costs."[22]

A much safer and more efficient procedure occurs when a physician simply logs into a computer and keys in a prescription like computerized order entry (CPOE). It is more efficient and much safer. Special diets, medication orders, lab tests and other procedures all should be computerized.

Electronic health records, computerized physicians' orders and paperless prescriptions are only a few of the visible steps currently being taken to improve our health care system.   Other steps in progress are image transfer technology, digitizing radiologic images, CT scans and MRI's and allowing for immediate transmission to electronic chart and the physicians' office!

Obesity is now a Crisis

We depend upon our trucks and our cars to take us from place to place, to get us to where we want to go. If the tires are low, we add air; if the oil is low, we add oil; if the engine is out of tune, we retune it. Generally speaking, we tend to do everything we can to keep these machines in working order so that they can provide us with the service we expect from them.

Unfortunately, that is not what we do for the machine we live in – our bodies… the machine we depend upon for life itself.

We eat fast and we consume a great deal. It is not so much what we eat but how much we eat. We consume an inordinate amount of fast food. We neglect to get a sufficient quantity of naturally nutritious foods such as fresh fruits and fresh vegetables (not canned), fresh poultry such as turkey and chicken (preferably not coated with a few tons of grease, oil and butter), fresh fish, an occasional steak and baked potato or baked sweet potato (not "low value" masked in a box) and fresh salads.

With exceptions, we make time to watch all of the athletic events but provide little time to participate in them. Our children have a fixation on the television – add pop corn, candy and a soda and you've got a great prescription for child obesity!

Our country has gone overboard with one diet or another, diet pills and diet plans, none work for everyone and few of them last – "losing weight" and "self-restraint" is not always compatible entities. Losing weight has become a national obsession. "The Center for Disease Control (CDC) announced in March, 2004, that poor diet and lack of exercise resulted in 400,000 deaths in 2000 and were about to overtake smoking as the number 1 preventable cause of death in the United States."[23]

A recent study found that more than 10% of U.S. children ages 2-5 are overweight. Obesity is on the rise. It's a risk factor for diabetes and it increases one's chance of having a life threatening heart attack or stroke.

It is unrealistic and unfair to expect severely obese people to use sheer willpower to fight the powerful genetic forces that drive them to put on pounds. The must seek medical attention.

Aside from medical advice, the logical antidote requires a great deal of restraint. We need to place greater emphasis on good health and proper nutrition. We need to promote it on billboards, on the radio, on TV, in our magazines, newspapers and in our theaters. We need to promote exercise and good eating habits similar to the way we promote the dangers of cigarette smoking. Our TV ads stimulate appetite. We need to encourage moderation and proper diet. We must raise nutritional awareness with ourselves and with our children.

Health Care Coverage and Insurance

Resolving our health care crisis will certainly require a great deal of debate – particularly as it applies to adequate insurance coverage for those who have not yet retired and likewise, for those who have and are now receiving coverage with Medicare under the Social Security program.

To make any headway, our lawmakers will need to take a bilateral political approach to the problems. Unproductive political rhetoric must be set aside in the interest of seeking a way to provide a better health care delivery system.

While lobbying in Washington is, and has been permitted, it must be in some way, controlled and not permitted to dominate the scene as is the case with the drug industry. Political payoffs and personal interests should not be tolerated. Likewise, the interests of "big money" or by tax rebates and/or unfair and unnecessary tax breaks for the wealthy.

A bilateral approach should be taken to discuss a free market system favored by the right and a national system favored by the left. A system should be built encompassing possibly some of each – a system which would best serve the changing American community.

Under one health care plan being proposed, people would be encouraged to own their own health plan. A system of health care savings accounts gradually phasing out employer provided insurance is advocated. To help offset the cost, a tax credit could be applied to either conventional insurance plans or to the purchase of low premium high deductible plans. Overall the plans are very complex and highly debatable.

A variation of this, with some added features might also be considered. The plan would generally include the following: (1) A mandate requiring employers of say 10 or more employees, to provide a fairly comprehensive health coverage plan which would include prescription drug coverage. The plan could even require a fairly high deductible to lower the cost to the employer. Family coverage could remain optional, but available at a much lower additional premium than normally charged or offered with employee participation – again very nominal.

(2) The employer would be entitled to a tax break somewhat greater than the normal tax deduction taken by businesses as an "employee benefit business expense deduction"!

Under this plan the employee is entitled to reduce the adjusted gross income on his/her tax return by the full amount of the employee's share of the insurance premium paid for health insurance coverage. This in effect reduces taxable income directly by the amount of the premium paid for the deductible. Ordinarily premiums paid for insurance are only allowed to be added to other medical expenses and applied to schedule A (the long tax form). Under this conventional method the total medical expenses are subject to calculation on the tax forms usually reducing the deduction substantially or in some cases voiding it altogether, but in either case, it's not a direct reduction of the gross taxable income as it would be under this plan. The difference is very substantial.

Every pharmacy manufacturer would be required to enter into contract with all major retail drug chains dispensing prescriptions. The contract would provide a substantial change in pricing policies. Thereafter, all pharmacies under contract with the manufacturer would pay a "contract rate" – a rate reasonable enough to make a profit, but low enough to enable the carrier to cover his cost. The federal government would also enter the picture by helping to cover some of the manufacturer's initial research and development costs: for example, an additional tax credit of some sort. The ultimate end result should satisfy everyone.

The manufacturer gets some of their initial cost from "additional" tax credits. The insurance carrier is compensated for reducing premiums and including prescriptions. The consumer now gets prescription drugs virtually free – but for a deductible cost which is used to reduce his taxable income.

In addition, the plan would call for an increase in the amount of gross wages taxable under FICA – increased to a maximum of $225,000. This would help to compensate the government for assistance to pharmacy manufacturers and will also decrease overall costs.

Some proposed changes in the offing are... free initial comprehensive physical exams for new medical beneficiaries, screening tests for cholesterol and diabetes for those already in the program.

A large portion of Medicare costs are due to those beneficiaries with multiple chronic diseases. These diseases are also among the most preventable. We need to better coordinate medical care.

A system involving a change from traditional Medicare to private run managed care (operated in regions throughout the country) is also being considered. But managed care (privately owned) is generally fraught with fraud and corruption throughout.

Hospitals are notorious for "over charging". In addition to the unreasonable high cost of drugs, hospitals are notorious for over charging especially on small items which are often overlooked. Doctors, likewise, although entitled to a just fee are charging outrageous fees for only a few minutes of dedicated professional time. It's understood that that they are faced with trying to compensate for equally outrageous malpractice insurance, but it is totally out of control. The physicians diagnostic and treatment codes should control most of this, but doesn't, due to so many instances of outright fraud even here! (Note: This could be controlled with more effective medical "administration" discussed elsewhere in this manuscript).

Another problem that seems to crop up from time to time is that of what constitutes a low-income family. The new Medicare drug discount program is a prime example of this. If a family is indigent or simply earning a very low income they, in most cases, qualify for Medicaid. However, the family earning $20-$40 thousand and in need of medication is left in a serious bind to keep pace with drug costs they simply cannot afford.

No one can deny that the crisis is a tough one – one not easily resolved. AARP in its December 2004 Bulletin surmised up measures they considered appropriate:

- Modernize Medicare
- Overhaul Social Security
- Change the way many Americans obtain health insurance
- Change the federal tax structure

Our politicians must set aside their differences and bilaterally come up with a workable solution in the best interest of the American public.

Medicare Coverage
Medical Coverage Available to You as a Medicare Participant

All Medicare participants should have a current official copy of "Medicare and You". It is available from the Centers for Medicare and Medicare Services (CMS). A copy is available by calling (800) Medicare (633-4227) or by visiting the internet at www.medicare.gov (TTY users should call (877) 486-2048). This is a U.S. Department of Human Services publication and it is quite comprehensive as applied to coverage under Medicare.

Before proceeding with any discussion of health cure alternatives and options available to you under Medicare – it is best to provide you with a simplified overview of basic Medicare.

Medicare's original plan (the basic plan) is divided into Part A and Part B. Part A covers inpatient care in hospitals, Hospice and home health care.

Part B covers medical services like doctor's services, outpatient care and other services which Part A does not cover. Part B is optional, although for most people in Part A, you must also enroll in Part B. In either case, it is highly recommended to participate in Part B; the payments (or premiums) are paid each month. If you are on Social Security, the premium is automatically deducted from your Social Security check.

People on the original Medicare plan are eligible to add drug coverage by enrolling in a Medicare prescription drug plan. These plans are now available through private companies that work with Medicare to provide prescription drug coverage. This is referred to as Medicare Part D.

For most of the services under Medicare Part B, you must pay a co-payment (or co-insurance) and a deductible may also apply.

"Medigap" Coverage Plans

These plans are provided by private companies at varying costs and provisions. They help pay for the co-insurance and deductible fees under Medicare. To help pay for many costs which the original Medicare plan does not cover, you might consider a Medigap policy. Medicare does not pay for these and they are generally referred to as "supplementary policies" or Medicare supplemental plans. Premiums for these plans will vary depending upon coverage. However, you must have Medicare Part A and B to participate. With Medicare basic coverage under Part A and Part B, you are still not covered for prescription drugs! That's a separate policy. For example, AARP has a Medigap policy insured by United Health Care. This is a good supplemental plan. AARP also offers a separate plan to cover prescription drugs called AARP "Medicare Rx Plan." These plans are good, as others may be, however, they are not free.

Medicare Advantage Plans: These plans are Health Care Management plans, like HMO's and PPO's. They are approved by Medicare and run by private companies. They are a part of the Medicare program referred to as Part C. However, their costs to you are separate and independent from Medicare. When you enroll in a Medicare Advantage plan, <u>you are still in Medicare</u>. Medicare Advantage plans provide all of your Part A (hospital) and likewise, Part B. The plans must provide medically necessary services. However, costs provisions will vary a great deal from plan to plan. A plan may offer additional benefits and may also include Part D coverage. It is important to note, however, that most of these plans have a physicians, hospital and clinic network, listing those who are participating in their plan. In most cases <u>you must use the physician, hospital or clinic listed in their network</u>.

Medicare pays an amount of money for your care each month to the private company you are enrolled with regardless of whether or not you use the service. Remember that you are still in the Medicare program with all rights and protections provided by Medicare.

These Managed care plans offer the promise of more effective care than you get through traditional Medicare. A managed care plan generally requires more counseling and testing with certain diseases or illnesses such as diabetes. This helps to avoid costly complications down the road. The care is generally better coordinated than that of routine fee for service care.

It is claimed that the government currently pays more for a patient in managed care than for one in traditional care. Of course this also shows that the insurers are profiting at the taxpayer's expense. As of February 2007, this issue is being currently debated by the government.

Each plan offers its fair share of inducements. Many, if not most, provide a plan with no monthly premiums. Some offer a plan with no deductible. The co-insurance (co-payment) fees will vary on medical coverage. Hospital stay charges and coverage will vary with each plan.

One plan offers you a choice of doctors with no fixed listing (network) of member doctors, hospitals, etc. Others require you to select from their network of participating providers. Some provide a form of dental care, some eye care or hearing care. Some plans require you to get a referral from your primary doctor before seeing a specialist – others do not.

The prescription (Part D) benefit may vary considerably from plan to plan. Some will provide generic (non-brand) drugs free of cost to you. In either case, the prescription you have filled are categorized by pharmacies as tier 1, 2, 3, etc. and depending upon the tier level of your particular prescription, your cost will be charged accordingly. Each plan has its own set of charges per tier number.

Some plans have what is called a "donut hole" – which is a coverage gap. After you have spent a certain amount of money for coverage drugs, (i.e. out of pocket), you have to pay all of the costs for drugs which are in the gap (the donut hole). Once you have reached another predetermined amount, your plan's "out of pocket" limit, you will have "catastrophic" coverage. When you reach this limit, you then pay only a very small co-payment for your prescriptions for the rest of the year. Some plans have a donut hole, some do not.

There are also plans which will agree to refund the amount you pay for the Part B premium.

Choosing the Right Plan for You: Obviously, these plans offer some very spicy incentives… do not be misled! Weigh carefully what may appear to be a decided advantage! Selecting the right plan to accommodate your particular needs is a challenge. Each of these companies offers impressive credentials and incentives. Do not be deceived. What's right for one person is not necessarily right for someone else! My suggestion is as follows:

Contact by mail, or e-mail, or call directly a good number of these plans such as Humana, Blue Cross, Mutual of Omaha, Secure Horizons, Advantage Care, Well Care, Universal, United, Freedom Health, to name a few. Have them send you their literature. Do not make any appointment with any of them yet – just get their literature.

Next, sit down and try to determine your medical needs using the previous year as an example. During the year… were you hospitalized? How often? How long? Did you have to go to an emergency room? Did you have surgery?

Were you in a hospital or clinic or had outpatient surgery? How often do you visit your primary (family) doctor? Per month? Per year? How often have you had x-rays? MRIs? CT Scans? Per month? Per year?

List all of the prescription medications you take. Go to your pharmacy and ask him to identify which prescriptions are generic. Which are tier I, tier II, etc. Any special medication? This is most important because different plans offer varying rates per each type of prescription... i.e. Tier or generic etc.

Try to come up with a synopsis of your medical needs. This will help you determine which plan is best for you. The benefits of each plan are different. You need to compare and see which fits your needs best.

It's a job but it's important. Before you make any decision, you may need to request assistance but not assistance from one of the plans. They want to sell you their plan. Only when you have a fairly good idea of what you need and which plan matches your needs best; then, and only then, call for an appointment with possibly one or two to make a decision... good luck!

This check list will help you with your plan comparatives.

- Is there a premium? Will the plan pick up your Part B premium?
- Is there a donut hole in their prescription plan?
- Be sure to ask for a copy of each plans' "network" (if applicable) so you can decide if your doctors are included?
- Will the plan cover you out of state? Out of country?
- What are the plans cost for inpatient hospital stays?
- Does the plan require a referral each time you need to go to a specialist?
- Check out the plans co-payment as they apply to medical services and pharmaceuticals.
- Will the plan provide mail service?
- Are their costs to visit your primary doctor or costs to visit the specialist?
- Conditions covering existing conditions?

There are other questions but this will get you going.

Please note that while a Medigap plan (as compared to an Advantage plan) may appear to offer more secure coverage (which it does in many cases). It is also far more costly than an Advantage plan. Remember with a Medigap plan you still pay the full Part B premium and a separate premium for the prescription plan… it adds up!

Inquire about changing plans if you decide to change and the time deadlines you need to meet to enroll.

Proposed Solutions

The cost of health care is growing at twice that of wages, driving up the price of insurance. In fact, a large percentage of recent bankruptcies can be attributed to prohibitive medical costs. Physicians fear being slaves of malpractice insurance. Uninsured patients are taken care of with the hospital absorbing the cost. These hospitals are struggling to break even.

Entirely too many illegal immigrants are receiving full medical care – of course out of compassion. Where, pray tell, is the money to come from? Both Medicare and Medicaid provide essential and commensurate service. However, both services are threatening to explode to keep pace with costs. In each case, we are compelled by ethics and compassion – not economics! Contradictions and inconsistencies in medical practice coverage are abundant.

The rapid escalation of insurance premiums with commensurate decreases in benefits, i.e., quality of care, is appalling. Congress is, and has been, debating over health care... how much to invest in medical research, how doctors are compensated, etc. Should we reduce the budget we have allocated to some medical services and what are our priorities? How does one prioritize the state of health of our citizens? Should we offer tax breaks for the employer or to the individual paying his own insurance? In either case, improving our health care system should be a top domestic priority.

Proposals for ensuring that Americans have access to health insurance are as follows:

- Individual tax breaks.
- Business tax breaks for covered employees' health care costs.
- Mandated business coverage for all employees.
- Expanding Medicare and Medicaid to cover everyone.
- Individual options to subscribe to Medicare or Medicaid programs.

Note, in each case, we still are faced with effective control, involving crime, fraud, abuse and corruption.

AARP in an article entitled, "Where Do We Stand" by William D. Novell, CEO, appearing in AARP's Magazine in February 2007, offers the following:

- Make affordable quality health care available to all Americans.
- Cut health care waste and inefficiencies to get more value out of the system.
- Make affordable prescription drugs available to everyone.
- Make prevention and wellness programs a priority.
- Provide affordable long-term care at home and in the community.
- Strengthen Social Security to guarantee our children and grandchildren can have adequate quality of life when they retire.
- Help workers save and have access to health retirement plans.

Universal health care, of course, remains a highly debated system option.

Space Age Technology and Techniques – "A Prognosis"

Surgeons will yield the proverbial "knife" less as new techniques with laser technology and radiation and drug therapy make today's operations obsolete.

Transplants and artificial implant operations will rise dramatically. Super drugs will also be developed to counteract acute pain, senility schizophrenia and depression.

In the not too distant future scientists will have the "know how" to (make) regenerate dead cells in the brain and in the spinal cord – bring hope for paraplegics and brain-damaged victims.

"Through diagnosis, treatment and correction of genetic defects, we will be able to prevent a load of genetic diseases that cause human suffering and impair the quality of life", says Victor McKusick, Chairman of the Department of Medicare at John Hopkins Center.

Gene therapy may manipulate personality, intelligence and physical appearances. Large companies are already offering health care "in house" (on site). It has its practical advantages.

Roughly 25-30 years ago this writer had the privilege of attending a medical seminar held in Bend, Oregon, on "Multi Phasing Screening". As the name implies it is a very sophisticated medical machine capable of "multiple diagnostics". This machine, after only a matter of less than an hour would generate a hard copy printout of your complete body system and functional diagnostics. At the time, as it was explained to us, the technology was great but not economically feasible. First, it would dramatically impact physicians in the field by virtually taking over the diagnostic process. Doctors would henceforth only perform the prognosis process of medical care and prescribe treatment accordingly.

Certainly physicians would lose a great deal of revenue. At any rate it was "floored" so to speak – replaced by bits and pieces of the technology – such as the MRI, the CAT scan and numerous others – each on their own merit.

We live in a fast changing dynamic environment. What the future holds may be a fascinating venture into the unknown!

PART V
OUR SOCIAL CRISIS

An Introduction

As man progresses technologically, he also changes socially. Modern communication itself highlights man's social issues to the point of crisis! Women's lib, gay couples, abortion, immigration, retirement and Medicare issues, to name a few, have each had a profound impact on our way of life. Now each of these is considered a real challenge, and in most cases, virtual crisis.

Changing Family Values
The Deterioration of the American Family

"The harsh reality is that the entire history of the human race from the present to the earliest written texts is an unbroken record of so-called patriarchy, presumably extending back at least as far as our early primitive ancestors. In every human society, without exception, leadership is associated with the male and the nurturing of children with the female."[24]

This bond of mother, father and child found in every society begins with marriage – the most universal social institution known – with father as the breadwinner and protector and mother taking care of house and children full time. Thus the man, the woman and the offspring form the institution we call "the family" and there is little doubt that this institution plays a vital role in our society.

We depend upon the family to provide social order, economic success, survival, and the development of our children and the emotional and physical health of each family member and the enforcement of society's values. Parents are expected to protect their children from the increasingly hostile environment, to recognize right from wrong and, last but not least, to "live and let live" and respect other human beings and their way of life even though it may differ from theirs. But the traditional family values are in the process of change… family values, as such, have declined dramatically with very adverse effects on children.

The cohesive group consisting of man, woman and child(ren) which was considered a family is becoming a thing of the past. Factors contributing to this sociological trauma are, to name a few, the changing place of women in today's economy, the recognition and acceptance of gay couples living together, the relative ease of divorce, split (separated) families living apart, the increasing mobility and economic instability (frequent career moves, etc.) of industry.

About 19 million or 1/3 of all American children lives apart from their fathers. Many of them have never visited their father's home. Typically they do not even see their father during their growing years. The amount of time spent with the children has dropped – in large measure due to both spouses working and distant grandparents and working mothers – and is here to stay.

Today's generation of children manifests these changes in many ways. Just to mention a few – maladjustment, excessive independence, lack of respect, delinquency, violence, suicide, substance abuse, eating disorders, stress problems and depression.

Materially, they appear better off today, on the surface, healthier and they do complete more school, although dropouts are still too prevalent.

The Women's Liberation Movement

The American Woman Suffrage Association (AWSA), led principally by Lucy Stone, Henry Blackwell and Julia Ward Howe, was formed in November 1869 in reaction to Susan B. Anthony's and Elizabeth Cady Stanton's establishment of the National Woman Suffrage Association in May 1869. The formal Declaration of the Rights of Woman was made on July 4, 1876.

These women (and Henry Blackwell) were convinced that once women achieved suffrage, they would use their ballots to participate in government and institute justice and economic equality demanding full rights of citizenship under the land.

Their boundless determination and their contribution of money, time and energy is evident in today's liberal society. In the years to follow, women continued their plight to gain recognition and equal opportunity – student revolts, women activists, demonstrations – meetings of professional associations demanding equal employment opportunity in a world previously dominated by men.

Women today expect to be treated equally, have plenty of opportunity and achieve more parity in family roles. The modern feminist movement has advanced the causes of women to the point where there are now more women in the workplace in the U.S. than ever before.

Professions and trades that were traditionally regarded as the province of men have opened up to women. Women now have easier access to education and training to excel. Women are found in increasing numbers among lawyers, judges and elected officials. We have women astronauts, women in police and fire departments and in the armed services. The province of women is now excluded nowhere!

Women make up 55% of current college grads. They win almost automatically in custody disputes. Victims of violent crimes are overwhelmingly male and wives assault husbands more frequently than the reverse.

Women in large numbers have rejected major aspects of their traditional role. Families have deteriorated and this deterioration of the traditional family structure affects men, women and children. On the one hand, the women's liberation movement can only be thought of in a very positive way – it was only fair – it was right – it was justified – no one can deny that. However, it has seriously impacted the social value of family. It was of course, an inevitable sociological change in today's modern society.

The Abortion Issue

The act of procuring or inducing a premature delivery and then the death of an offspring, called abortion has been practiced since ancient times. It is currently a religious, political, and social issue. Does the woman or the government decide?

Judaism, having a high respect for family, for women and for individual life, had condemned abortion in Biblical times, but found certain exceptions to it. Then, as Christian belief began to crystallize, condemnation of abortion came to an almost absolute value. As Professor John T. Noonan of the University of California at Berkley says in his book, "it eventually identified into an extremely firm and certain moral opinion."[25]

Proponents and opponents of abortion rights are highly polarized leaving little ground for compromise. Abortion is generally defined as the expulsion of a fetus of an unborn child from a pregnant woman's womb before the fetus is ready to live outside the womb.

In the light of today's advanced knowledge of embryonic and fetal development modern science contends that life begins at fertilization.

A baby's heart begins to beat between the eighteenth and twenty-fifth days. The brain begins to function as early as forty days into pregnancy. How about when conceived in the womb – i.e., does conception constitute life? Others contend that a baby in the womb is not a baby at all. It is only a fetus. Those against abortion say that the fetus is indeed a separate genetic entity – a human being of the homo sapien species – one of us. They contend that it is a crime of the first order to abort a living organism – a baby.

A woman has certain (not total) rights to her baby but not over another living human's body just because he or she happens to live inside her. This analogy says it well… "I have the right to swing my fist at you but that right stops at your nose!"

If abortion is wrong, then mother and baby should be protected unless it can be shown that one's life (the mothers) might be lost if the pregnancy were allowed to continue.

Only the preservation of one life is weight enough to justify taking another. This, of course, is a viewpoint of some people.

Illegal abortions have often been performed under less than adequate medical standards – thus greatly increasing the risk of harm to the woman.

Political debate continues in Congress over provisions to cover abortion. Various measures are introduced, challenged and then contested or revised to include the privacy rights of minors. But no firm resolutions have yet stood the test of satisfying all concerned.

Pregnancy from rape is reputed to be extremely rare as a reason for legalizing abortion, rape and incest. These illegal acts are often used as nothing more than an emotional screen by those profiting from abortion. But we must approach the victim of rape or incest with great compassion. She needs love, support and help. She has been the victim of a violent act.

We have a right to freedom of religion but not if that religion involves human sacrifice. A woman has a right to her body but this new being growing within her is not a part of her body – rather this is a totally different human being – so says the opposition to abortion.

Some say we shouldn't impose morality on the owner (the mother) for she has the constitutional right to choose. Clearly, this is a woman's rights issue. The question is should she or should she not have the right to choose? Women contend that without the right to control their own reproduction, they could not fully realize other rights.

Welfare abortion is another bone of contention. A large majority of people do not want to pay for welfare abortions. Is it cheaper to abort or to support another welfare case?

In view of the seemingly untenable position of both sides of the issue, it would appear as though there is no solution which will satisfy everyone. However, a reasonable course of action might be considered to alleviate some of the tension. For example:

(1) If a woman is raped or becomes a subject of incest and subsequently becomes pregnant as a result of the unjust act, it should be appropriate and perfectly legal for her to take the relatively new non-surgical abortion pill, the RU 486, Mifepvistone or Mifeprex (steroid hormones) to stop the gestation of an early pregnancy. It must be taken in the first seven to nine weeks from the first day of the last menstrual period. RU 486 is an FDA approved product to end pregnancy.

(2) If a pregnant woman wishes to tough it out and carries her baby to term, there can be good memories, her own child to love and cherish or if she is in no position to parent her child, she can put her baby for adoption in a pair of lonely arms of a couple unable to have a child of their own. The cost, however, should be incurred by the state under welfare.

(3) If, due to extenuating circumstances, a natural pregnancy occurs but the mother is not well and cannot medically tolerate an abortion which could possibly place her life in jeopardy, then either the RU 486 application or a surgical abortion may be in order and should be permitted by law – as a matter constituting a legal burden on the mother.

The abortion issue is indeed a medical, theological and scientific problem of the first order and, of course, directly and or indirectly impacts family values and marriage.

The Gay Impact on Marriage

Today, we have an additional force at work to further erode and possibly even destroy what we know as the traditional institution of family – namely the predisposed gay people.

Most people would agree that all members of a just society should have equal rights under the law. They should not have to endure the harassment and discrimination that the gays and lesbians often experience. At any rate these people have had a significant impact on family values here in this country.

If gays or lesbians want to live together, let them do so, that certainly is no crime, but not as a married couple living together in holy matrimony. It has been customary in this country, and in most other countries throughout the world, to define marriage as a union between a man and a woman. This country was founded on Christian Judeo principles. Most of our founding fathers believed in the sanctity of marriage as an institution between a man and a woman.

Some view the attribute of a gay or lesbian as inborn – that the individual had no choice and they were born that way. Others contend that is not so, but thus their traits are developed. In either case, the option to prefer a same sex partner is dominant with either one. The option to have a bisexual relationship may be possible but not with the same emotion and feeling. This is, of course, is only what I have understood to be the case.

What has developed here is the claim that the gays have made. They claim that if people of the same sex become married or claim marriage they should be entitled to the same rights and privileges as any other married couple.

Several states have attempted to establish a base on "same sex" marriage despite the efforts of gay rights activists. A number of states have succeeded in contesting and overriding the laws, which recognize gay (same sex) marriages. In some states marriage is legally undefined. It becomes a real controversial issue. Most states remain opposed to same sex marriages.

Gay couples fear marriage bans would affect their benefits. Certainly there are ways to extend benefits to gays living together without the marriage certificate. Viewing gay couples as a legal entity for certain legal benefits should be considered. We do the same for certain unmarried couples (heterosexual) living together today and meeting a (time together) time criteria.

If however, the gay movement takes hold and marriages of gay couples are approved everywhere – normal propagation of our species would certainly be affected.

For all practical purposes, the government does not have the power to stop two people from exercising their right to marry. Denying marriage privileges because of homophobia is wrong.

The constitution does not mandate that married people have a fundamental right to tax benefits or visitations in a hospital or special insurance treatment. We're talking about privileges here – not rights!!

According to some, the "committed" homosexual couple is entitled to the same legal benefits as a married heterosexual couple.

Committed generally implies couples who would get married if they could; it likewise, means that the couples vow before their god, state or community that they intend to remain together forever "until death do us part".

Mixed couples have to sign a marriage license to validate the marriage. No matter how committed a same sex couple is, if one person wants to adopt the other person's last name, a civil action is required; whereas, none is required with a heterosexual couple. What the state confers upon people is a civil action... and it should be conferred on any couple committed enough to want to be treated as a unit by the state.

I think there are good first amendment reasons to reserve the term marriage for religiously sanctioned unions. However, we need to create a new term for civil sanctioned ones – at least until society is ready to recognize all types of unions as marriages.

For legal documentation, general speech and religious circles, marriage has different ramifications, thus the utility of the term "civil union" for same sex types.

A proper approach for the time being would be legislation that defines and differentiates between the two, i.e., a marriage and a civil union. It should indicate the steps necessary to comply for civil union status.

If a couple desires to enter into a civil union type of relationship (a civilian sanctioned partnership) it should enter into a prenuptial agreement stating just how a separation would be handled relating to the property and assets the couple have enjoyed together. Adults wanting to dissolve a relationship want to do so with as few strings as possible. This contract would resolve many problems and possibly enable the power to be (the state) to grant the privileges normally just granted to married couples.

Step 1... a written legally documented civil court approval for civic union status.

Step 2... a prenuptial agreement. Legal issues that affect couples such as interstate succession, consent to health care, income taxation, division of property etc. could then be considered for approval.

Traditional marriage is God's design for the family and it is rooted in Biblical truth. However, like so many things today, it has become disputed as a religious and philosophical matter, not to mention the legal implications it involves.

For all intents and purposes, the state has no business telling the church what marriage means – but the church, by the same token, has no business telling the state what it means in lieu of legal implications.

The question is what kind of family environment is best for the health and development of children, and, by extension, the nation at large since the children of today are the adults of tomorrow.

Divorce, death, abandonment and unwed pregnancy result in many single parent families. Children should have a mother and a father. Each one contributes a different essential quality to a child. A man may contribute justice, fairness, duty, a sense of right and wrong and of course, physical attributes, i.e., the masculinity of man; whereas, a woman will contribute hopefulness, sympathy, care, grace, patience and love.

Decades of research have produced a consensus among social scientists of both right and left persuasion, that "family structure" has a serious impact on children.

Adolescent, single-parent families are more likely to have a child who would pull a knife on you and become involved with a gang. Generally speaking two biological parents have children who fare better than in any other family types. Unfortunately, diverse family forms are here to stay. Of course, the term "marriage" has been used for over a millennium and it is not going to disappear from public view.

PART VI
SOCIAL SECURITY

Overhauling Social Security

Most everyone agrees that our Federal Income Tax system needs overhauling. The tax code is very complex and in many ways penalizes the working poor and the middle class, while rewarding the super rich with plenty of loopholes and tax shelters, allowing some to avoid paying anything.

Of course, our Social Security system is an integral part of this complex tax system as applied to payrolls and other income received throughout our country for work performance.

People are living longer and in the near future there will be more retirees collecting benefits than there are workers paying into the systems. The question is whether or not the current system can handle the retirement of "baby boomers" – nearly 77 million of them born from 1946 through 1964! Not to mention the generations to follow! Actuaries and congressional budget analysts agree that the system could be kept solvent for at least the next 75 year. Obviously, we need to take steps now to keep the system solvent.

Not long ago, President Bush stated that in 2018, the Federal Retirement System will start paying out more in benefits than it collects in taxes! "Today's system is unsustainable!"

Discussions which followed, took this impending "thunderbolt" to task. Those in opposition claim "fear tactics" were being employed although most agree that the system is in need of some fine tuning. Most agree that today's system is not economically sustainable indefinitely. Some maintain that it quite possibly could manage to pay 100% of the money guaranteed to beneficiaries until at least the year 2042. Even after 2042, nearly 75% of the benefits could be paid until the end of this century.

Social Security is the promise our country makes to working Americans for their retirement. It's true it needs to be strengthened but not replaced. We cannot afford to weaken our Social Security and place benefits for future generations at risk. Social Security is the only thing that keeps 40% of America's seniors out of poverty.

Today, not only do two-thirds of all seniors rely upon these guaranteed benefits as their primary source of income, but so do 4.8 million widows and widowers, 5 million disabled workers and 38 million children of deceased workers depend upon Social Security. This, according to a publication for members entitled "What You Need to Know about the Future of Social Security".

President Bush has advocated that we overhaul the Social Security program. He wants to revamp it by letting younger workers divert some payroll retirement contributions (taxes) into "private investment" accounts. Each individual decides how he or she chooses to invest it. (It is assumed here that it would be mandatory to invest the money. Otherwise, if optional, too many would opt to simply spend it – it's only natural!

By investing we turn every American into an investor, rewarding individual initiative and judicial risk; however, that sounds like radical conservatism.

Currently these withheld contributions (taxes) are invested in government securities. The amount withheld is matched by the employer. Under the proposed system, the employer would stand to benefit from the cost of the employee matching contribution. However, it would have to be assumed that the individual employee would be required to make the investment as opposed to simply spending the money.

If the individual doesn't invest wisely, or if the market drops, a major problem could occur, placing the individual's retirement fund in jeopardy. It is very risky for the two-thirds of the seniors who rely on Social Security for their main source of income and this applies in particular to women who, more than men (currently), depend upon their Social Security for their retirement.

These private accounts would drain resources for retirees faster and would also reduce Medicare benefits. Investment companies (i.e. Wall Street) would, of course, stand to gain from the fees charged for their services.

The cost to make the transition to the private investment account system is estimated at up to $2 trillion – a burden on our already growing budget!

According to Polk, a substantial 40% of American adults support private accounts; however, when told how much the transition would cost, most would have a change of heart. When asked to weigh the risks of investing and paying out management fees, the opposition rises.

A national "sales tax" as an option needs to be explored also. A so-called "value added tax" (used by some other nations successfully) should also be considered.

Thumbnail Sketch of the Fair Tax
A Comprehensive Plan to Replace Income and Payroll Taxes

"The Fair Tax proposal is a comprehensive plan to replace federal income and payroll taxes, including personal, gift, estate, capital gains, alternative minimum, Social Security/Medicare, self-employment, and corporate taxes. The Fair Tax proposal integrates such features as a progressive national retail sales tax, dollar-for-dollar revenue replacement, and a rebate to ensure that no American pays such federal taxes up to the poverty level. Included in the Fair Tax plan is the repeal of the 16th Amendment to the Constitution. The Fair Tax allows Americans to keep 100% of their paychecks (minus any state income taxes), ends corporate taxes and compliance costs hidden in the retail cost of goods and services, and fully funds the federal government while fulfilling the promise of Social Security and Medicare.

"No federal sales tax up to the poverty level means progressively like today's tax system. To ensure no American pays tax on necessities, the Fair Tax plan provides a prepaid, monthly rebate (prebate) for every registered household to cover the consumption tax spent on necessities up to the federal poverty level. This, along with several other features, is how the Fair Tax completely untaxes the poor, lowers the tax burden on most, while making the overall rate progressive.

"No tax on used goods. The amount you pay to fund the government is totally visible. With the Fair Tax you are only taxed once on any good or service; the sales tax is charged just as state sales taxes are today. If you choose to buy used goods – used car, used home, used appliances – you do not pay the Fair Tax."

Fair Tax is a service of "Americans for free taxation" – a more partisan grassroots organization dedicated to replacing the current tax system. The above thumbnail sketch is a copy, taken from their printed material received in the mail. They can be reached at 1800-FairTax.

This plan certainly has many favorable aspects and it has stimulated a great deal of interest. Of course, there are pros and cons to be debated – not everyone agrees it is the way to go.

It is interesting to note here that "the average income of the top 10% of American taxpayers rose 88.6% from 1970 to 2000 – from $119,249 to $224,877 per year."[26]   This represents a sizable potential source of funding for Social Security if the "cap" on payroll contributions could be raised and used to keep the system in order.

William D. Novelli, Chief Executive Officer of AARP, suggests "restoring total wages taxable by Social Security to 90% of nationwide earnings. This would move the cap from $90,000 in 2005 to $140,000 phased in over a decade. This would lower the projected shortfall by some 43%"[27]

It is appropriate to mention here that it should not be necessary to cut Medicare benefits as indicated elsewhere in this manuscript. Medicare needs to be streamlined, wastes reduced, errors eliminated, corruption and disruptive politics corrected. This alone would cover a large part of the total problem.

President Bush has also recommended another tax rebate. This may appear to be in order to stimulate the economy but how does one justify that rebate applying to those earning over $250,000 a year? Simply because we live in a free and equal society where what applies to one applies to all – "just doesn't cut it." Sure these people earned it, but there are extenuating circumstances governing what's right, when so many people cannot even afford reasonable living conditions. And so many cannot afford the cost of essential health care with particular reference to medications – especially for those who do not qualify for welfare (Medicaid); yet require a number of very costly medications they just cannot afford.

Likewise, our cost of living increases in benefits are usually dissipated by the hike in Medicare Part B premiums and the increasing costs of health care.

According to corporate America, we had over 112,000 pension plans in the year 1985. Over 60% of these plans are no longer in force. After the "Enron" debauchery, not to mention other disasters which followed, one wonders how much confidence and trust we can place in corporate pensions and savings plans!

Likewise, the Government Accounting Office reports that mortality rates among different racial groups suggests that black (African Americans) are more likely to die before receiving a retirement benefit than their Hispanic or white counterparts. The higher death rate is reflected in the large percentage of African American children receiving Social Security benefits. Therefore, simply raising the retirement age would raise another problem.

In conclusion, we have a number of options to consider:

- Should we raise the cap to 90% of taxable earnings?
- Should we simply increase the payroll tax rates?
- Should we increase the taxes on benefits?
- Should we extend coverage to state and local government employees (it's newly hired)?
- Should we adopt the Fair Tax plan?
- Should we consider President Bush's plan of "private savings accounts"?
- Should we increase the national retirement age to 70?

- Should we cease paying benefits to affluent retirees who really do not need any assistance?

The author agrees with AARP in that the individual retirement savings accounts as an option, in addition to our Social Security plan, but it is no solution.

Likewise, your writer agrees that raising the cap on wages subject to the Social Security tax has merit. This would raise the taxable level above the current rate to assure that everyone shares in a more equitable manner.

Whatever the ultimate resolution is, our Social Security system must prevail and provide not only retirement cash benefits, but peace of mind as well!

PART VII
THE ENERGY CRISIS

An Introduction

We are at war on at least two fronts. Terrorism continues to rear its ugly head, threatening us at every turn. Family values have found their way out of the back door of convention. We are in a plight to provide a good health care system for everyone, despite corruption and the skyrocketing costs to provide it equitably and in an arena fraught with political dissention. We are attempting to come up with a sound practical retirement system to replace the system we have. Our present system is on very tenuous economic grounds with a debatable future. We are struggling with an immigration program which appears to be out of control. If this isn't enough of a quandary to deal with, a major energy crisis is facing us, which fuels our very economy and could quite possibly seriously impact our very lives in the not too distant future.

In the past 100 years, we have made phenomenal progress in science, industry and technology. This has enabled us to build huge industrial complexes and shopping centers and make vast improvements in agriculture and Medicare. Materials have undergone vast changes. We have plastics and aluminum. We have an aerospace industry. Of course, we also enjoy television, radio, telephones and our gas guzzling big cars and trucks and, of course, nuclear energy.

We pride ourselves on our accomplishments and justifiably so. These same accomplishments have, however, been realized by utilizing vast quantities of the earth's resources and they require even greater quantities to use them. The resources I refer to are our fossil fuels such as coal, gas, oil, etc. The use of these fuels, however, may have created a very subtle yet possibly disastrous effect. I refer here to the carbon dioxide emissions which could conceivably contribute to what we now refer to as "global warming"!

The cars we drive, our gas guzzlers, are responsible for a large amount of these emissions. Therefore, our auto industry has been asked to seek out more fuel-efficient gas-guzzlers or find ways to replace gas as the fuel to run these autos. Our dependence upon foreign sources to supply us with the gas and oil compounds the problem. Of course, large industries also use these fossil fuels in the manufacturing process; consequently, they too are responsible.

Nor can we rely on the alternative sources of energy available to us, such as windmill turbines, which are helpful but not adequate. Solar energy is another possibility, which is an effective source, but far from being accepted universally as yet. Nuclear power has decided advantages, but its waste is toxic and it has no life span. We haven't fully developed clean nuclear energy. Ethanol, a product taken from corn sounds good, but it could produce as many problems as it may solve. Natural gas and hydro power are also considered alternatives; however, they have not been fully developed for use as yet.

Environmental fears have created their own set of problems as applied to our forests and possible offshore drilling and oil deposits.

We seek fuel efficiency while attempting to accommodate our demand for more gas guzzlers. One car alone is not sufficient to satisfy most American families. Consequently, our roads are over crowded. Traffic moves slowly with a great deal of congestion in the downtown areas. Accidents take place when we are in a hurry or on our cell phones or perhaps, we have had too much to drink. Parking is a major problem in so many of our cities – large or small.

Despite all of this, we refuse to invest in what is and has been available for some time. I refer of course to a more economical, safer and far more convenient means of transportation – namely – transportation within our metropolitan areas such as the monorail, the tram, and fast city-wide rail systems like the one in Portland, Oregon. These systems are far more practical and would resolve a major portion of our gas/oil and gas emission problems.

Cities like Los Angeles have petitioned for this for years to no avail. There is a solution for distance driving as well but that will take longer to implement. I have made reference to this at the end of this energy section under "What the Future Holds".

I once lived in Chicago Heights, Illinois, near the border of Indiana. Each day, my neighbors and I would get into our little putt-putts and drive a couple of miles to a parking lot, where we would pick up our tram to Chicago. The tram ran from Chicago Heights to downtown Chicago in just 38 minutes. We boarded, found our seats and settled down to read the paper or play cards – going and coming. It was an enjoyable ride without care or concern – no gas, no hassle, safe, sound and economical!

What's to prevent us from developing these practical and convenient modes of transportation? In most cases the answer is politics involving big industry. That is, the steel industry, the rubber industry, the auto industry, etc. They will not encourage these methods of transportation for fear of losing revenue. They could, of course, diversify as the cigarette industry has done.

It is indeed a "crisis"– a conundrum. We want more, not less, we do not welcome change – we like our pretty gas guzzlers.

Oil and Gas

The price of oil and gasoline has been volatile and will probably continue to be so. International politics and economics are devastating enough without the terrorists who have made their intentions clear with attacks on oil workers and oil facilities in various strategic locations throughout the world.

It is not the supply of oil alone that is not meeting the demand, it's more complicated. It is extremely difficult to access and deliver to an increasing number of consumer's across the globe. We are paying dearly for our dependence on oil from other nations. The demand has in recent years increased dramatically with the two most populous nations in the world, China and India. China alone has about 1.3 billion citizens and tens of thousands of factories which run on stand-alone diesel/oil generators which gobble fuel. India does very much the same.

Saudi Arabia is a despotic regime using its vast resources to support a corrupt form of living for its many royal princes.

They live it up with the best of conveniences and pleasures while they inspire their young to hate us.

At any rate, Saudi Arabia carries the most weight in the "cartel" known as OPEC (the Organization of Petroleum states). It controls what happens to the availability and price of oil. About 85% of the world's petroleum is found in eight OPEC countries that Saudi Arabia dominates.

Iraq has a great potential for producing millions of barrels a day. It could even be considered the world's leading producer of oil. Of course it is not functioning well due to its internal factions at war with each other and the coalition states.

Can ethanol resolve the problems? Ethanol is an alcohol, distilled from fermented mashed grain. Its use would, most certainly, represent a "boon" for American farmers.

Ethanol consumes a lot of corn. It would place a strain on our meat prices and food supply in general. Likewise, environmental static would appear, resulting from the need for more land.

Actually ethanol is only slightly better for the environment as far as "greenhouse gases" are concerned, the growing and refining process would, however, use pesticides, fertilizers which all-in-all could create more of a problem than it would solve.

Perhaps we can produce ethanol from other natural products. Most experts agree that it will take an array of renewable energy technologies to replace fossil fuels. In any event, we need to make our factories and equipment more energy efficient.

Global Warming

There are catastrophic changes taking place from the North Pole to the South Pole. We have experienced heat waves and periods of unusually warm weather. Our planet's uniquely beautiful glaciers are melting, sea levels are rising and coastal flooding is taking place, sea ice is melting and the Greenland Ice Sheet is undergoing radical changes. The Gulf Stream currents are undergoing a change. Changes in climate are now affecting physical and biological systems on every continent.

Atmospheric changes, ice mass loss, and the like, may not be due to natural causes alone. While it is true that cyclical or periodic changes in the forces of nature do account for many climate changes, authoritative studies on the subject suggest that there is strong evidence that the climatic changes may also be caused by the burning of fossil fuels such as coal, natural gas and oil and gasoline to power our cars, factories, utilities and appliances.

Gases that trap in the atmosphere are often called greenhouse gases. Some greenhouse gases such as carbon dioxide occur naturally and are emitted to the atmosphere through natural processes. Other greenhouse gases (e.g. fluorinated gases) are created and emitted solely through human activities.

"The principal greenhouse gases that enter the atmosphere because of human activities are:

- Carbon dioxide (CO_2) – fossil fuels, solid waste, trees and wood products.
- Methane (CH_4) – emitted during the production of coal, natural gas and oil
- Nitrous Oxide (N_2O) – emitted during some agricultural and industrial activities.
- Fluorinated Gases – industrial processes use hydro-fluorocarbons, per-fluorocarbons and sulfur and hexafluoride."[28]

Scientists predict that problems will increase if these emissions of heat-trapping gases are not brought under control. "A new system has been developed to track carbon dioxide in the atmosphere. The plan is to be able to measure CO_2 regionally to help determine where it is being absorbed such as by trees and crops and where efforts to reduce release are or are not working."[29]

Of course cutting greenhouse gas emissions within the foreseeable future is not likely – not without some very strong legal sanctions to mandate compliance.

"The greatest damage may come in ocean and coastal eco-systems, water resources and coastal settlements. Water may become a scarce commodity on many continents affecting billions of people."[30]

Global temperature is projected to increase anywhere from 1.4 to 5.8° C until the year 2100. But it may vary widely depending upon regional responses.

Global mean sea levels have been rising at an average of 1 to 2 mm per year over the past 100 years which is significantly higher than the rate over the last several thousand years. Some reports say that sea levels could rise 7-23 inches.

"Our entire climatic system is fundamentally driven by energy from the sun; and the sun's energy output could vary, the earth's position in relative to the sun (our orbit) also varies slightly." [31]

El Ninos are not caused by global warming although El Ninos have been present for hundreds of years (some indications suggest millions of years). El Ninos have been more frequent and intense in recent decades due to a variety of causes.

Transforming the world's energy system from fossil fuels to clean energy is, of course, a tremendous task. It will require decades of work and trillions of dollars in an effort to reduce harmful emissions. It is referred to as geo-engineering.

The Greenhouse Effect

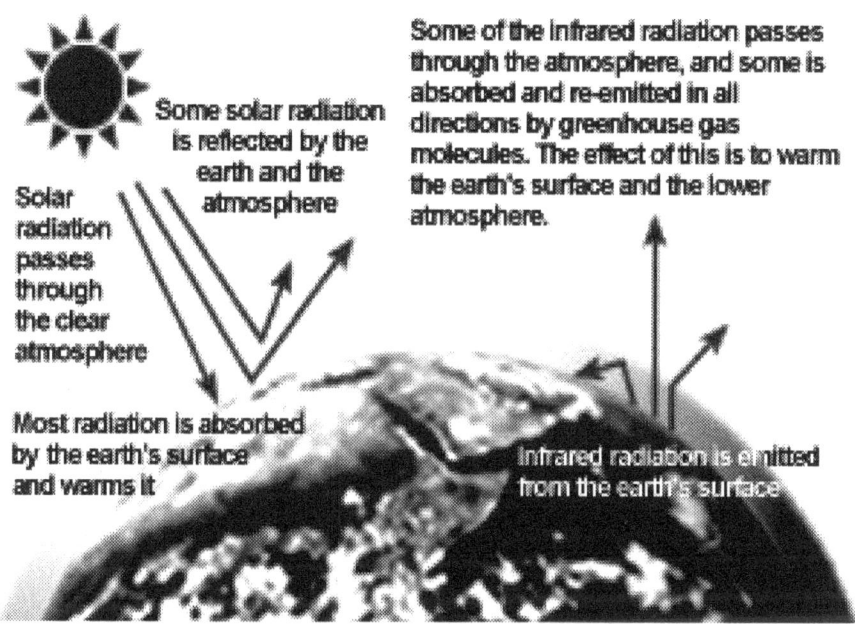

Source: Intergovernmental Panel on Climate Change (IPCC), the National Academy of Sciences (NAS and the U.S. Climate Change Science Program. Data described from the monitoring and analysis of NOAA, NASA and the Department of Energy.

What Does the Future Hold?

Our huge consumption of the earth's natural resources is paving the way for global warming and resource starvation in the predictable future.

We must make changes. Unfortunately, most people will procrastinate, "Oh there's plenty of time for that" or "It can wait" or "Let the future generations take care of it"... but, the problem is now, its urgent and it will not wait.

The demand for energy is outstripping our ability to supply it. It is a world wide condition, not just a problem for the United States alone. It could, in time, even threaten the existence of the human race.

Even fresh water is already critically scarce in most poor nations. Its abundant use in agriculture is already approaching its limits. War and disease may take their toll... survival of our existing energy crisis could conceivably take us out entirely!

We may even have to leave our planet someday to survive. That is not simply science fiction. We are already exploring other planets for possible resources and or life conditions.

Needless to say, the expenses we incur in wars in Iraq, Afghanistan and elsewhere, would go a long way in our pursuit of survival. Here again, we alone cannot do it. It will take a collective effort on the part of many nations working together.

On the more positive side, the outlook could be more promising… solar systems are one of our best bets as a safe economical resource. The development of hydrogen fuel for transportation would help tremendously.

In the future we may be able to use orbital satellites, working in space to provide our electric needs. NASA is currently working on a sunshade concept. Likewise, we may develop huge forests with artificial trees to reduce carbon dioxide emissions. All in an effort to engineer a solar planet to slow climate change. The experts say halting greenhouse emissions is our only real solution.

The sooner we develop more practical intercity and suburban transportation the better. Miami has a monorail system, Portland utilizes an effective in-town, fast rail system with periodic stops at conveniently located parking lots – it works! Modern airports use these rail systems. Chicago has, for years, used its rail transportation and it saves energy. But we must expand the use of these modern systems to reduce the dependence on auto transportation.

Somewhere down the road we will eventually have roads which may be electronically controlled. Each automobile is equipped with electronic devices which will attach to the long distance roads of the future. For example, once on the special highway, you set your auto's computer to the desired destination and off you go – no gas, no hassle, no traffic jams – virtually trouble free and very fast. If this isn't futuristic enough, envision, if you will, what is referred to as "rolling roads", similar to the rubber transportation found in airports today but obviously much more technologically advanced.

Our office buildings and restaurants and shopping centers will be free of any traffic, no cars or trucks, no parking lots and no smog. You get there from a fast tram; you arrive at a very beautifully landscaped area with parks which will accommodate all of your needs for business, service or pleasure. These cities may be a good distance from where you live, but with "ultra modern" modes of transportation. You can come and go in less time than before without the hustle.

Underground delivery systems using huge pneumatic pipelines will transport food, clothing and other essentials to the appropriate location within the city.

Believe it or not we have the technology. Of course we cannot simply tear down what we have. We will build in new areas and rebuild from within in others – it will take time.

Then again, we could take the domestic approach and simply bottle the energy generated by 3 or 4 small, healthy, strong children as they play in their playground.

BIBLIOGRAPHY

1. Axelrod, Alan, – Chronicle of Indian Wars from Colonial Times to Wounded Knee, 1952

2. Hirshfelder, Allene, Kreipede, Martha, – The Native American Almanac, A Portrait of native America Past, 1993

3. Gottesman, Ronald, – Violence in America, An Encyclopedia (Vol. 1), 1999

4. Thompson, Gale, – The Hispanic Almanac, A Reference Work, 3rd Edition

5. Napt, Jay Robert, – Terrorism in the 20th Century, Chicago, 1998

6. Maddex, Robert L., – International Encyclopedia of Human Rights, Freedom, Abuses and Remedies, 1942

7. Duncan, Meloa J., - The Complete Idiot's Guide to African American History

8. Hakim, Joy, - A History of the United States Reconstruction and Reform, Book 7, 1865-1870

WORKS CITED

[1] Gollesman, Ronald – "Violence in America" Vol. 1, An Encyclopedia 1999

[2] Hirschfelder, Arlene, Kreide de Montano, Martha – A Portrait of Native America", 1993, The Native American Almanac

[3] Hirschfelder, Arlene, Kreide de Montano, Martha – A Portrait of Native America", 1993, The Native American Almanac

[4] Michaels, Marquerill Shawnee – "A Trust Betrayed", Time Magazine, January 2004

[5] Thompson, Gale – "Hispanic American Almanac", a Reference Work, 3rd Edit

[6] Thompson, Gale – "Hispanic American Almanac", a Reference Work, 3rd Edit

[7] Goldberg, Jeffrey – "The Making of a Terrorist", the N.Y. Tribune magazine, June 2002

[8] Goldberg, Jeffrey – "The Making of a Terrorist", the N.Y. Tribune magazine, June 2002. "Looking Evil Right in the Eye", U.S. World and News Report, pg 87, July 26, 2004

[9] Wiesel, Eli – Novel Prize Winner, "How Can We Understand Their Hatred?" parade Magazine, pg 4, April 7, 2002.

[10] Zvckevman, Mortimer B. Editor-in-Chief – "A Shameful Contagion" U.S. News and World Report, October 7, 2002

[11] Flame, "The Saudi... Are They Our Friends... or Our Enemies?" Facts and Lies about the Mid-East, U.S. News and World Report, September 9, 2002

[12] Goultney, Bruce and Brad Rogers-editorial, Star Banner, July 27, 2004

[13] Dr. Rosenfield, 1 Sadore – We Must Fix Health Care, Parade Magazine, August 15, 2004

[14] Star Banner – Opinion Section (Health System Crisis) "Straight Talk about Health Care", February 22, 2004

[15] Star Banner – Opinion Section (Health System Crisis) "Straight Talk about Health Care", February 22, 2004

[16] AARP – "Snapshots", November 2004

[17] AARP – "Snapshots", November 2004

[18] Gage, Richard, "Society" – If You Live to be 100 – it Won't Be Unusual, U.S. News & World Report, May 9, 1983

[19] AARP – "Snapshots", November 2004

[20] Star Banner – Science & Medicine, Tuss, October 14, 2004

[21] Sherman, Mork – "Medicare Payment Errors Near $20 billion in 2003", Associated Press Writer, Star Banner News, December 2004

[22] Turner, Rob – "A High Cost of Tech", U.S. N & W R, Special Edition, August 2004

[23] Lemunick, Michael D. – "The Year, Obesity", Time Magazine, December 27, 2004

[24] Shaeffer, Robert – "Feminism, the Noble Life" Free Inquiry, Spring 1995

[25] Willke, Dr. and Mrs. – "Why Can't We Love Them Both?" Impose Morality.

[26] Johnston, David Cay – author of "Perfectly Legal", page 31, appearing in the Opinion section of the Ocala Star Banner, January 23, 2005

[27] AAR Bulletin, February 2005

[28] United States Environmental Protection Agency – "Greenhouse Gas Emissions", 2007 Draft

[29] Nesmith, Jeff – "Gore Implores Congress to Save the Planet"; Washington – "New System Tracks Carbon Dioxide"

[30] "Borenstein, Seth – "Warming May Usher Drought, Disease" Star Banner, March 2007

[31] National Environmental Satellite Data and Information Systems (NESDIS); NOAA Satellite Systems; National Oceanic Data Commission; Department of Commission US.

About the Author

Your author has a background covering over 50 years of experience in business management and health care administration. He is married with three children, six grand children and four great grandchildren.

He served in WW II in the Pacific Theater at the very end of hostilities. He earned his Bachelor's Degree in Business Administration and later a Master's Degree in Health Care Administration.

His career began in small business management and later provided financial and administrative services for medical clinics and physicians. Later serving as an acute hospital financial controller and then as a nursing home administrator where he was licensed in two states.

He traveled extensively and when retired, became a part time faculty instructor at a local community college. Currently, he resides in Florida.

www.ingramcontent.com/pod-product-compliance
Lightning Source LLC
Chambersburg PA
CBHW061346280526
45784CB00001B/154